YU THE GREAT

CONQUERING THE FLOOD

A CHINESE LEGEND

GRAPHIC UNIVERSE™

STORY BY
PAUL D. STORRIE

PENCILS AND INKS BY
SANDY CARRUTHERS

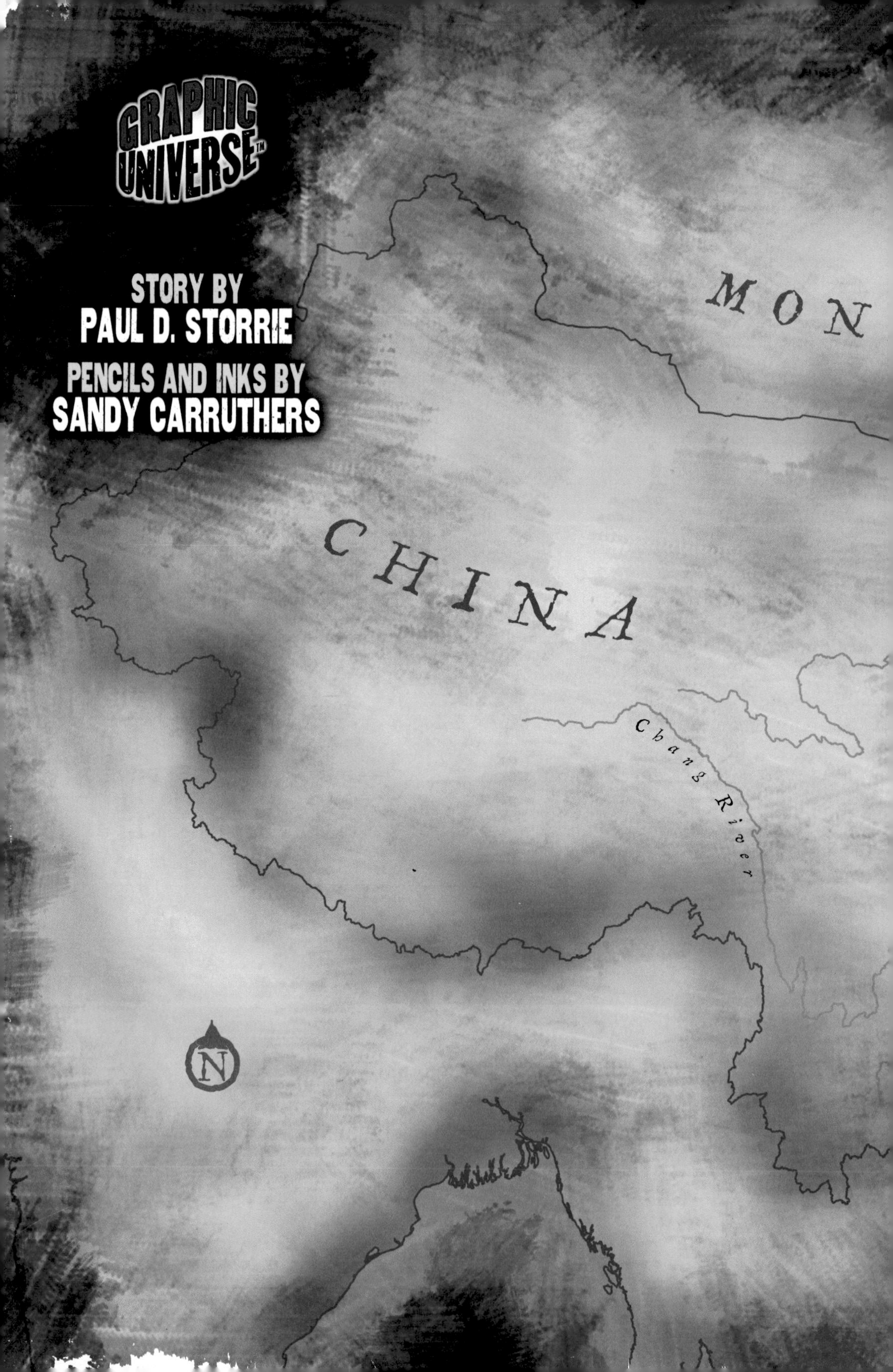
MON
CHINA
Chang River
N

YU THE GREAT

CONQUERING THE FLOOD

A CHINESE LEGEND

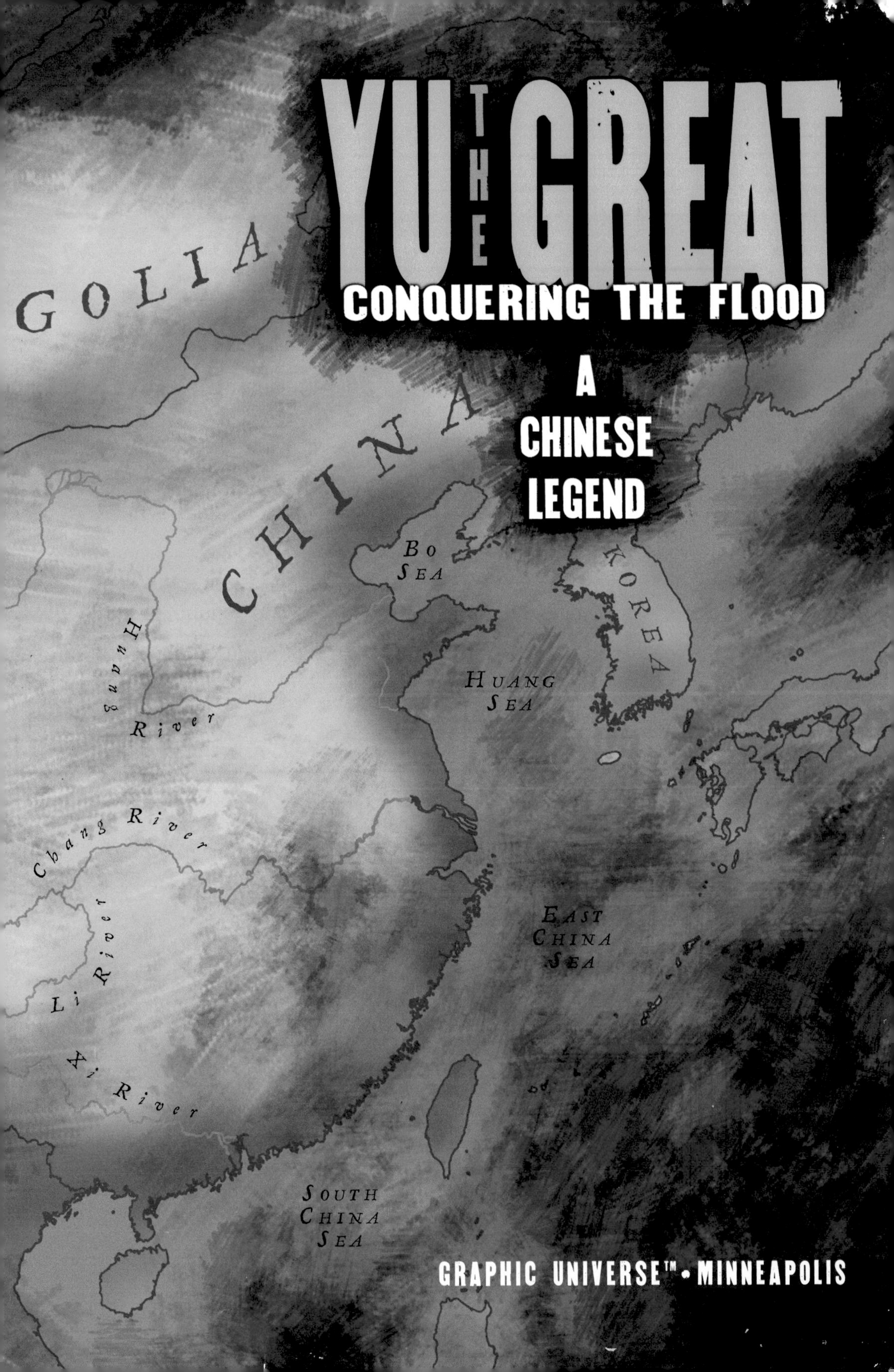
GOLIA
CHINA
BO SEA
KOREA
HUANG SEA
Huang River
Chang River
Li River
Xi River
EAST CHINA SEA
SOUTH CHINA SEA

GRAPHIC UNIVERSE™ • MINNEAPOLIS

Yu the Great: Conquering the Flood tells the legendary beginning of the Xia Dynasty (ca. 2100–1700 b.c.) of China. The Xia Dynasty is the first Chinese empire (family of rulers) described in historical records. Yu is considered the first Xia emperor (ruler). Yu's life story has fictional parts, but he may have been a real person. Some later Chinese texts describe Yu as a kind and strong emperor whose building projects saved China from frequent floods. *Yu the Great* draws on *Land of the Dragon: Chinese Myth* (edited by Tony Allan), *An Introduction to Oriental Mythology* (by Clio Whittaker), and other text sources, as well as many historical art resources, including more modern Manchurian elements, to make Yu a Chinese hero for the ages.

STORY BY PAUL D. STORRIE

PENCILS AND INKS BY SANDY CARRUTHERS

COLORING BY HI-FI DESIGN

LETTERING BY BILL HAUSER

CONSULTANT: WANG PING, MACALESTER COLLEGE

Graphic Universe™
An imprint of Lerner Publishing Group
241 First Avenue North
Minneapolis, MN 55401 U.S.A.

Website address: www.lernerbooks.com

Library of Congress Cataloging-in-Publication Data

Storrie, Paul D.
    Yu the Great : conquering the flood / by Paul D. Storrie ; illustrations by Sandy Carruthers.
        p.   cm. — (Graphic myths and legends)
    Includes bibliographical references and index.
        ISBN-13: 978-0-8225-3088-6 (lib. bdg. : alk. paper)
        ISBN-10: 0-8225-3088-0 (lib. bdg. : alk. paper)
        1. Folklore—China—Juvenile literature. 2. Da Yu, Emperor of China, d. 2197 B.C.—Folklore—Juvenile literature. I. Carruthers, Sandy. II. Title. III. Series.
    GR335.S712 2007
    398.2'0951'02—dc22   2005001524

Manufactured in the United States of America
1 2 3 4 5 6 - JR - 12 11 10 09 08 07

TABLE OF CONTENTS

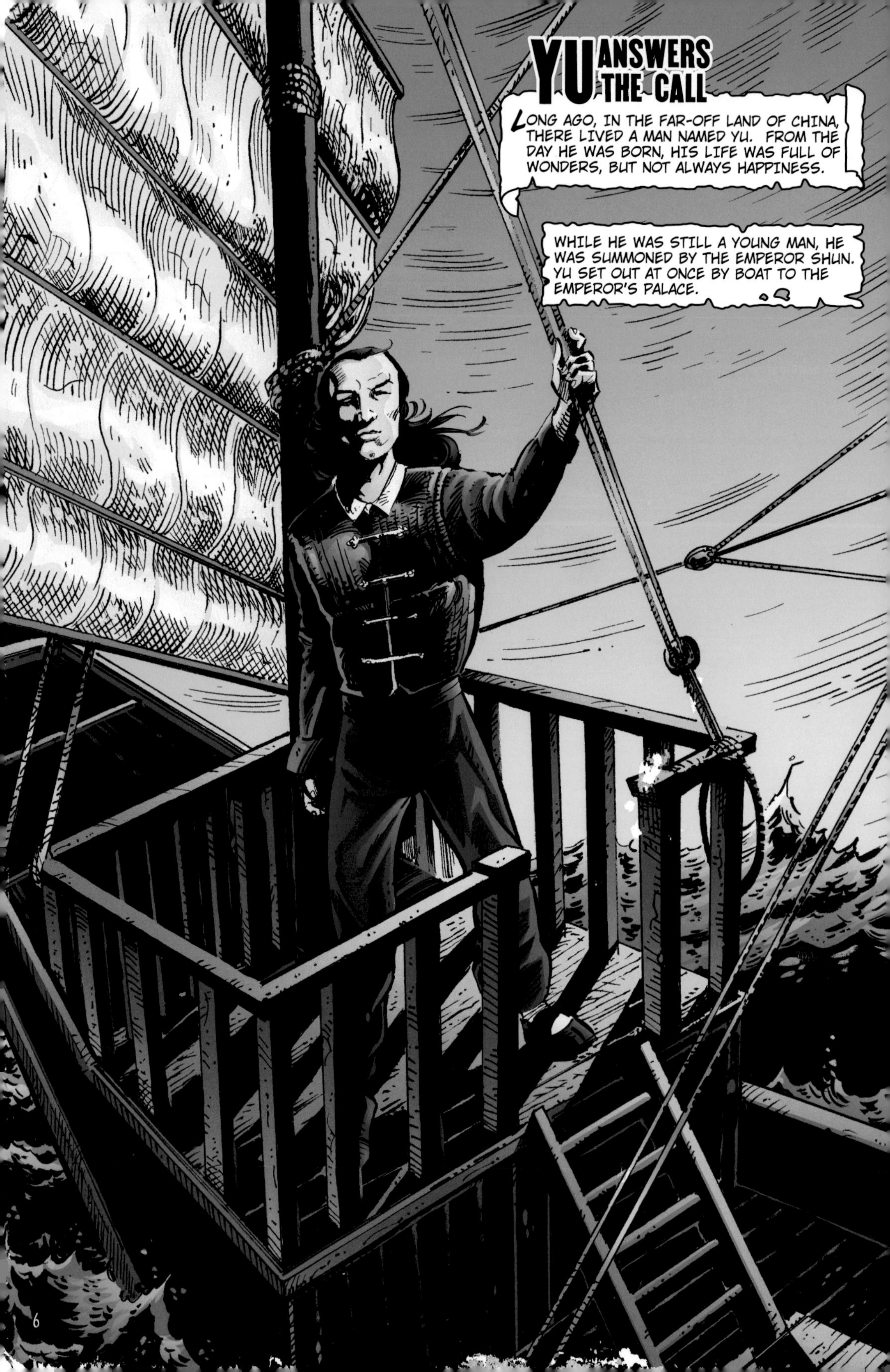
YU ANSWERS THE CALL
LONG AGO, IN THE FAR-OFF LAND OF CHINA, THERE LIVED A MAN NAMED YU. FROM THE DAY HE WAS BORN, HIS LIFE WAS FULL OF WONDERS, BUT NOT ALWAYS HAPPINESS.
WHILE HE WAS STILL A YOUNG MAN, HE WAS SUMMONED BY THE EMPEROR SHUN. YU SET OUT AT ONCE BY BOAT TO THE EMPEROR'S PALACE.

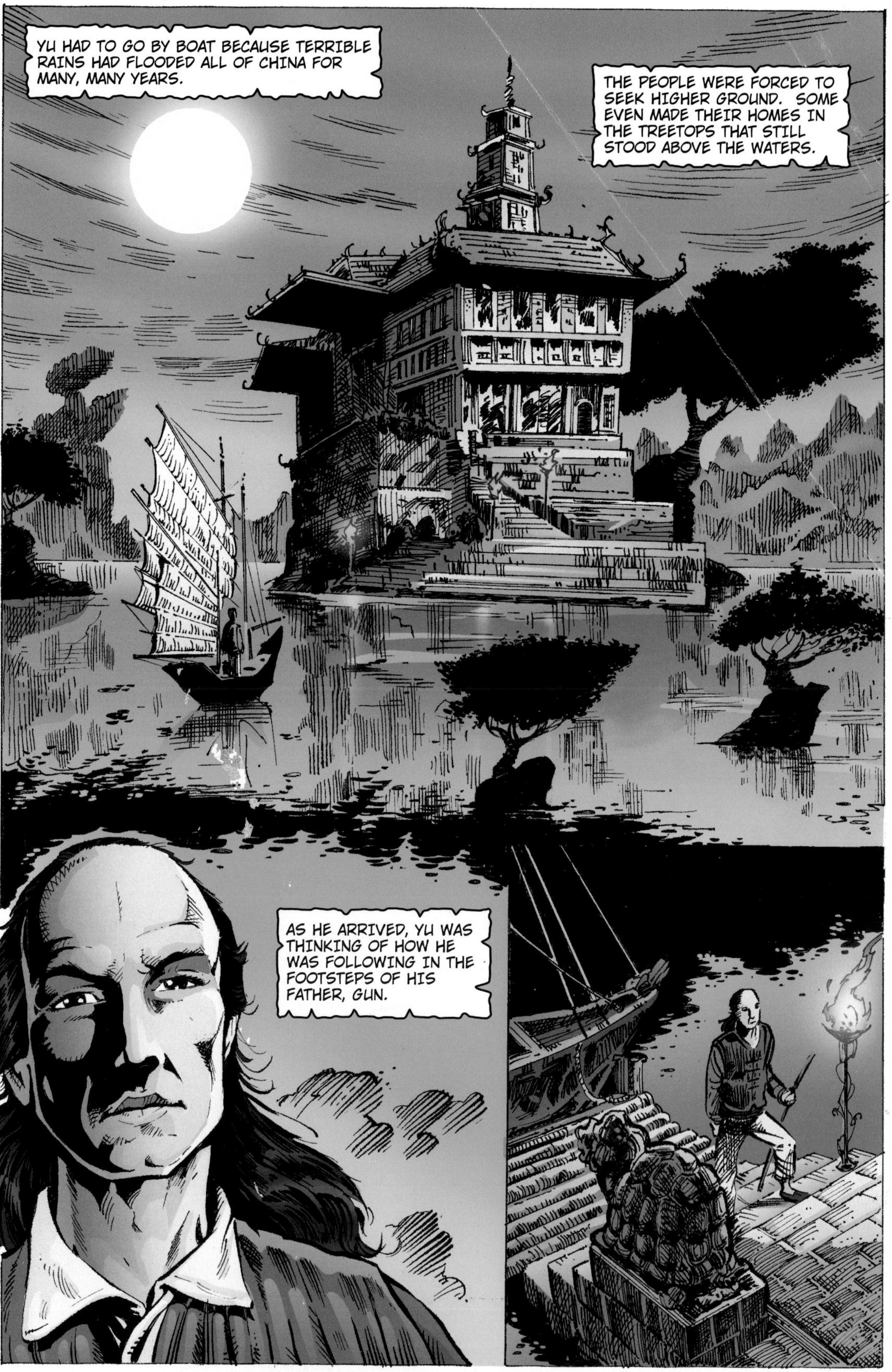
YU HAD TO GO BY BOAT BECAUSE TERRIBLE RAINS HAD FLOODED ALL OF CHINA FOR MANY, MANY YEARS.
THE PEOPLE WERE FORCED TO SEEK HIGHER GROUND. SOME EVEN MADE THEIR HOMES IN THE TREETOPS THAT STILL STOOD ABOVE THE WATERS.
AS HE ARRIVED, YU WAS THINKING OF HOW HE WAS FOLLOWING IN THE FOOTSTEPS OF HIS FATHER, GUN.

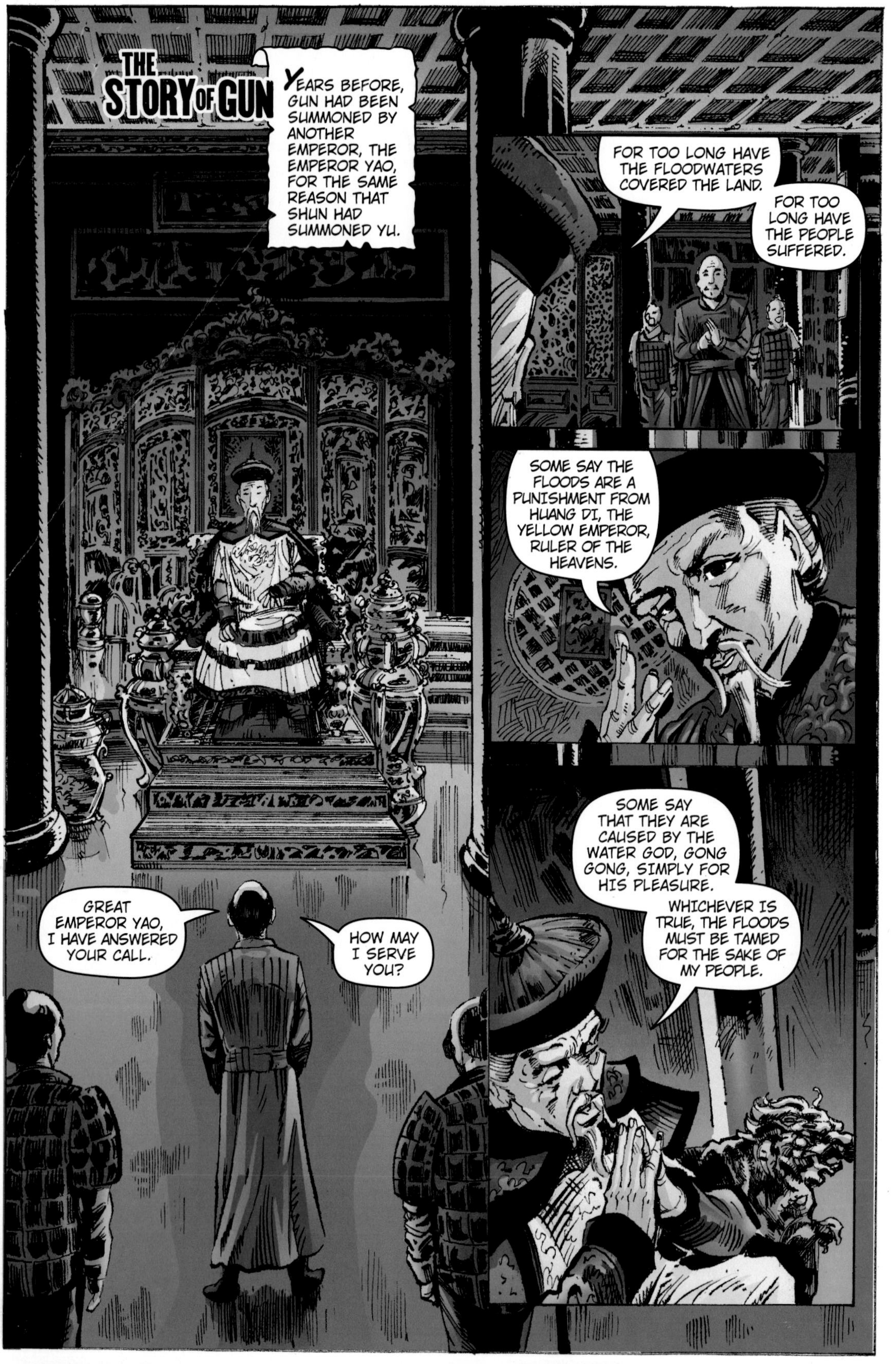
THE STORY OF GUN
YEARS BEFORE, GUN HAD BEEN SUMMONED BY ANOTHER EMPEROR, THE EMPEROR YAO, FOR THE SAME REASON THAT SHUN HAD SUMMONED YU.
FOR TOO LONG HAVE THE FLOODWATERS COVERED THE LAND.
FOR TOO LONG HAVE THE PEOPLE SUFFERED.
SOME SAY THE FLOODS ARE A PUNISHMENT FROM HUANG DI, THE YELLOW EMPEROR, RULER OF THE HEAVENS.
SOME SAY THAT THEY ARE CAUSED BY THE WATER GOD, GONG GONG, SIMPLY FOR HIS PLEASURE.
WHICHEVER IS TRUE, THE FLOODS MUST BE TAMED FOR THE SAKE OF MY PEOPLE.
GREAT EMPEROR YAO, I HAVE ANSWERED YOUR CALL.
HOW MAY I SERVE YOU?

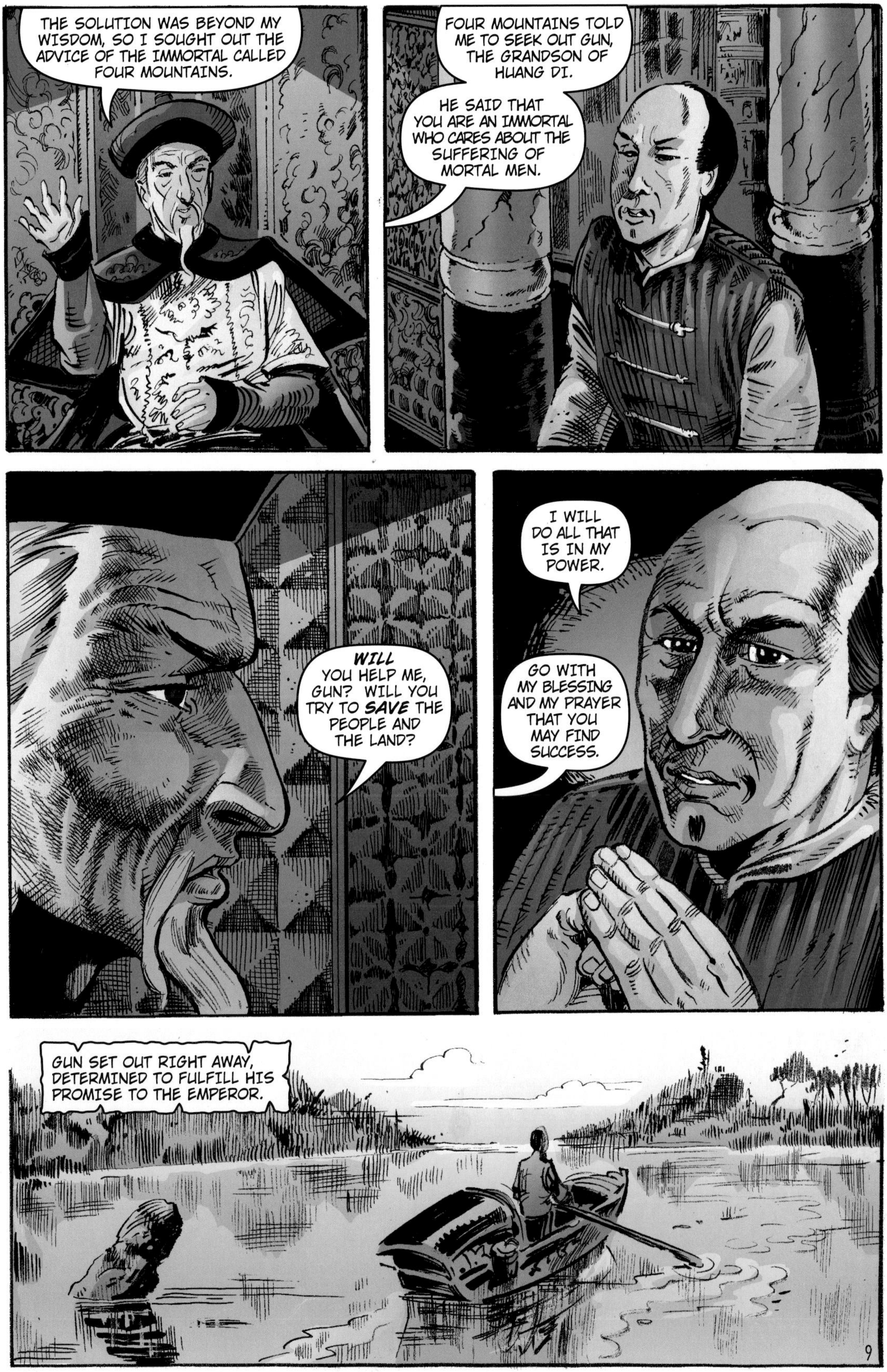
THE SOLUTION WAS BEYOND MY WISDOM, SO I SOUGHT OUT THE ADVICE OF THE IMMORTAL CALLED FOUR MOUNTAINS.
FOUR MOUNTAINS TOLD ME TO SEEK OUT GUN, THE GRANDSON OF HUANG DI.
HE SAID THAT YOU ARE AN IMMORTAL WHO CARES ABOUT THE SUFFERING OF MORTAL MEN.
WILL YOU HELP ME, GUN? WILL YOU TRY TO SAVE THE PEOPLE AND THE LAND?
I WILL DO ALL THAT IS IN MY POWER.
GO WITH MY BLESSING AND MY PRAYER THAT YOU MAY FIND SUCCESS.
GUN SET OUT RIGHT AWAY, DETERMINED TO FULFILL HIS PROMISE TO THE EMPEROR.

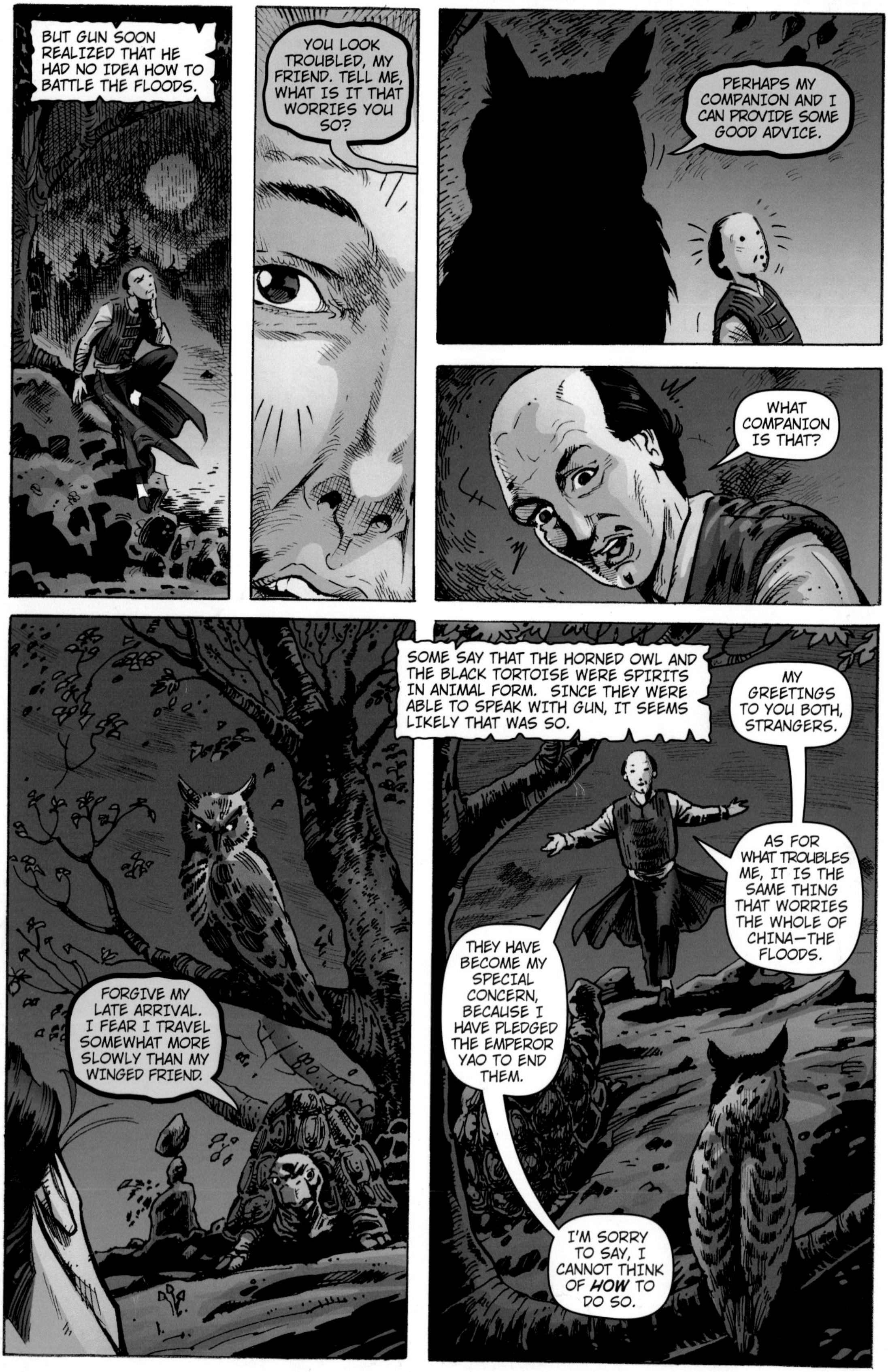
BUT GUN SOON REALIZED THAT HE HAD NO IDEA HOW TO BATTLE THE FLOODS.
YOU LOOK TROUBLED, MY FRIEND. TELL ME, WHAT IS IT THAT WORRIES YOU SO?
PERHAPS MY COMPANION AND I CAN PROVIDE SOME GOOD ADVICE.
WHAT COMPANION IS THAT?
FORGIVE MY LATE ARRIVAL. I FEAR I TRAVEL SOMEWHAT MORE SLOWLY THAN MY WINGED FRIEND.
SOME SAY THAT THE HORNED OWL AND THE BLACK TORTOISE WERE SPIRITS IN ANIMAL FORM. SINCE THEY WERE ABLE TO SPEAK WITH GUN, IT SEEMS LIKELY THAT WAS SO.
MY GREETINGS TO YOU BOTH, STRANGERS.
AS FOR WHAT TROUBLES ME, IT IS THE SAME THING THAT WORRIES THE WHOLE OF CHINA—THE FLOODS.
THEY HAVE BECOME MY SPECIAL CONCERN, BECAUSE I HAVE PLEDGED THE EMPEROR YAO TO END THEM.
I'M SORRY TO SAY, I CANNOT THINK OF **HOW** TO DO SO.

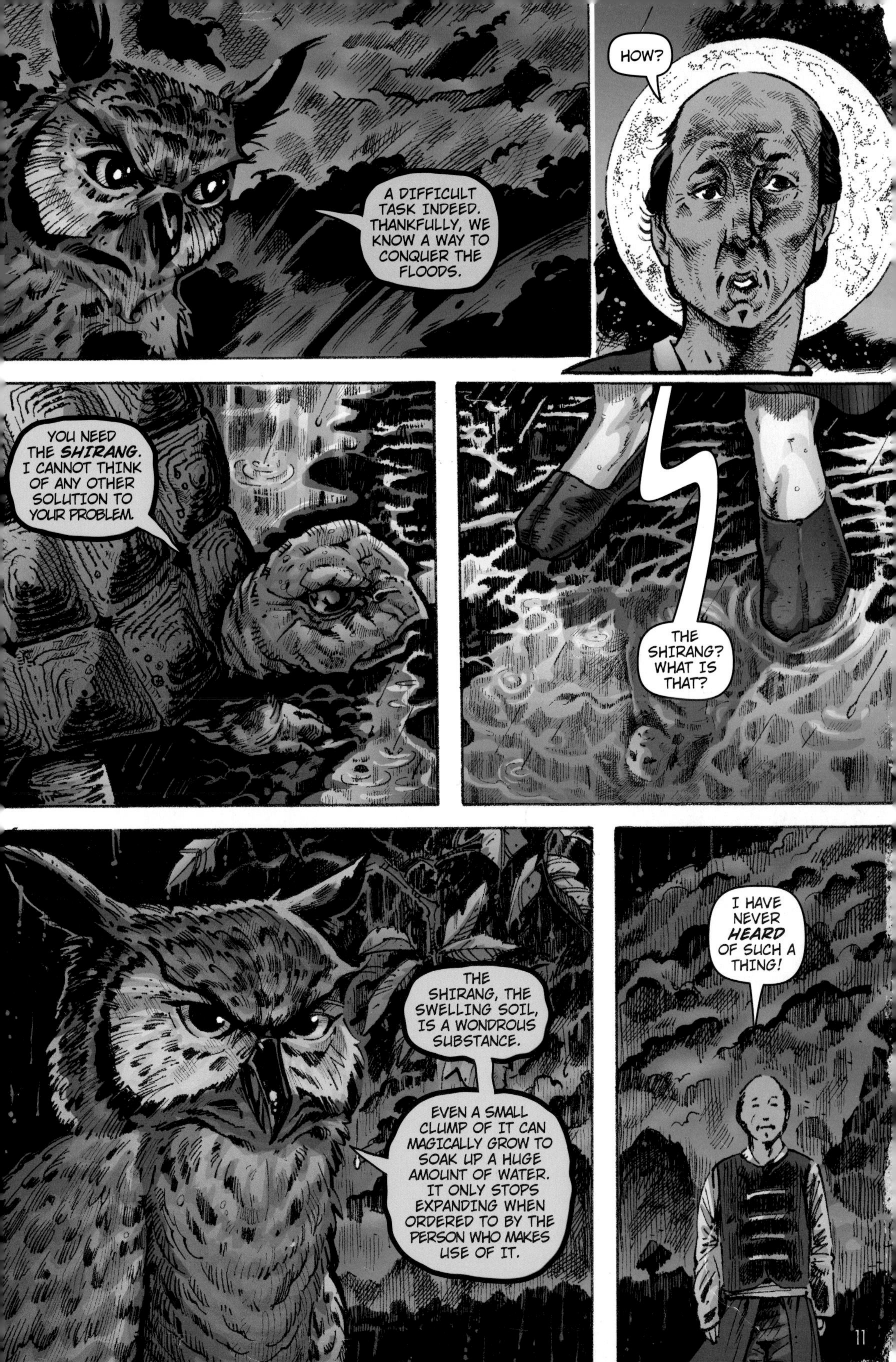
A DIFFICULT TASK INDEED. THANKFULLY, WE KNOW A WAY TO CONQUER THE FLOODS.
HOW?
YOU NEED THE ***SHIRANG.*** I CANNOT THINK OF ANY OTHER SOLUTION TO YOUR PROBLEM.
THE SHIRANG? WHAT IS THAT?
THE SHIRANG, THE SWELLING SOIL, IS A WONDROUS SUBSTANCE.
EVEN A SMALL CLUMP OF IT CAN MAGICALLY GROW TO SOAK UP A HUGE AMOUNT OF WATER. IT ONLY STOPS EXPANDING WHEN ORDERED TO BY THE PERSON WHO MAKES USE OF IT.
I HAVE NEVER ***HEARD*** OF SUCH A THING!

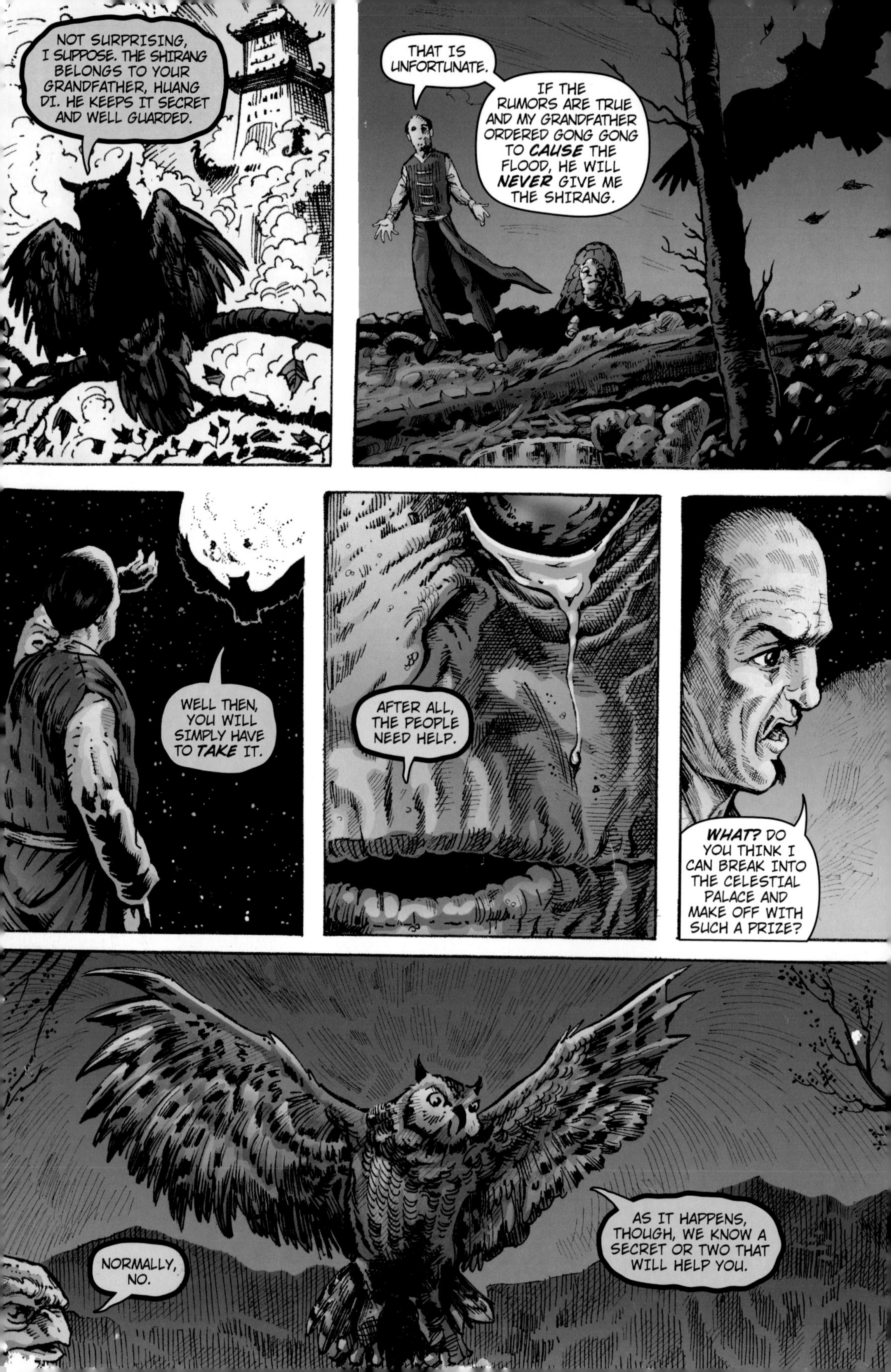
NOT SURPRISING, I SUPPOSE. THE SHIRANG BELONGS TO YOUR GRANDFATHER, HUANG DI. HE KEEPS IT SECRET AND WELL GUARDED.
THAT IS UNFORTUNATE.
IF THE RUMORS ARE TRUE AND MY GRANDFATHER ORDERED GONG GONG TO *CAUSE* THE FLOOD, HE WILL *NEVER* GIVE ME THE SHIRANG.
WELL THEN, YOU WILL SIMPLY HAVE TO *TAKE* IT.
AFTER ALL, THE PEOPLE NEED HELP.
WHAT? DO YOU THINK I CAN BREAK INTO THE CELESTIAL PALACE AND MAKE OFF WITH SUCH A PRIZE?
NORMALLY, NO.
AS IT HAPPENS, THOUGH, WE KNOW A SECRET OR TWO THAT WILL HELP YOU.

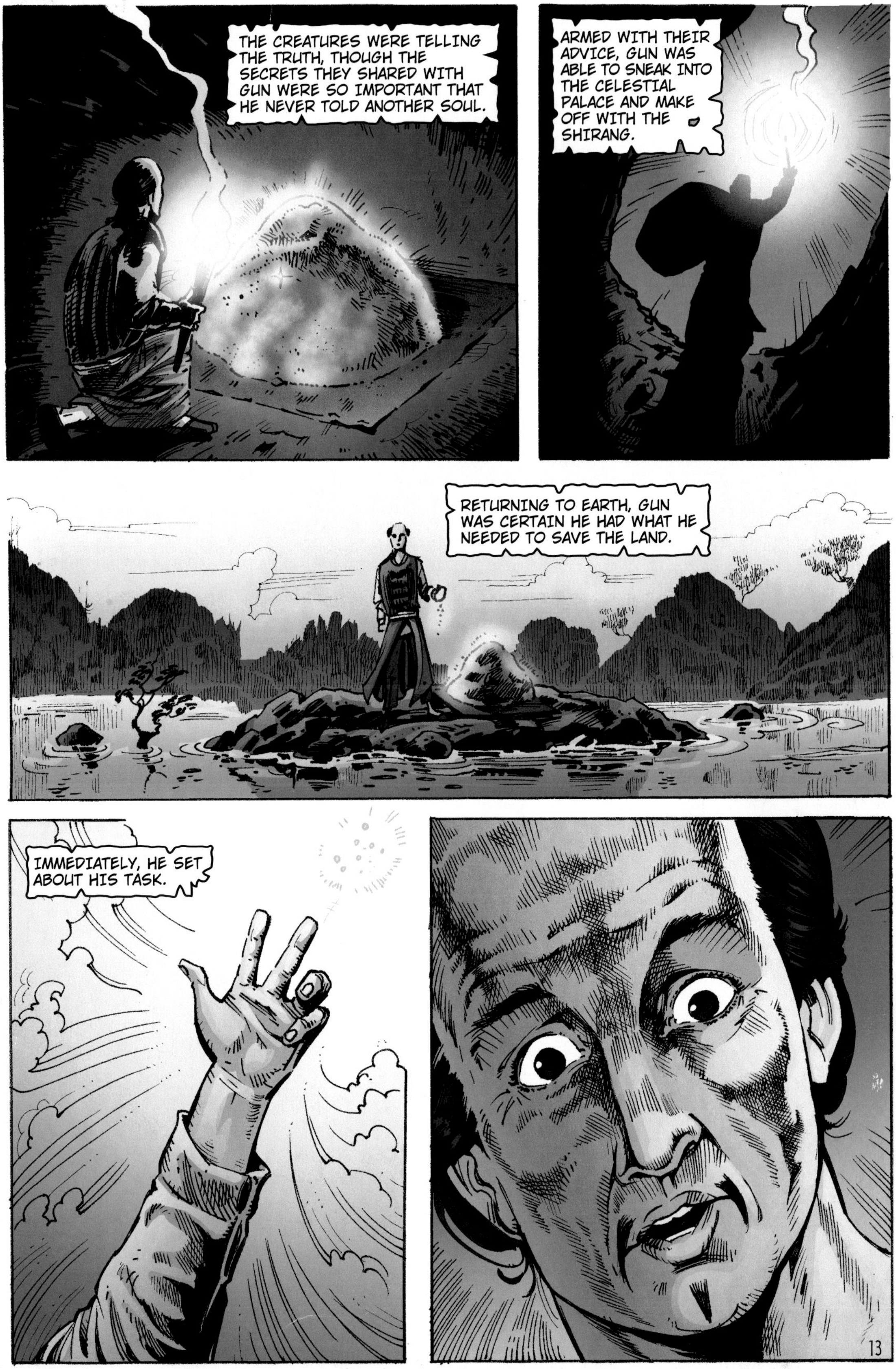
THE CREATURES WERE TELLING THE TRUTH, THOUGH THE SECRETS THEY SHARED WITH GUN WERE SO IMPORTANT THAT HE NEVER TOLD ANOTHER SOUL.
ARMED WITH THEIR ADVICE, GUN WAS ABLE TO SNEAK INTO THE CELESTIAL PALACE AND MAKE OFF WITH THE SHIRANG.
RETURNING TO EARTH, GUN WAS CERTAIN HE HAD WHAT HE NEEDED TO SAVE THE LAND.
IMMEDIATELY, HE SET ABOUT HIS TASK.

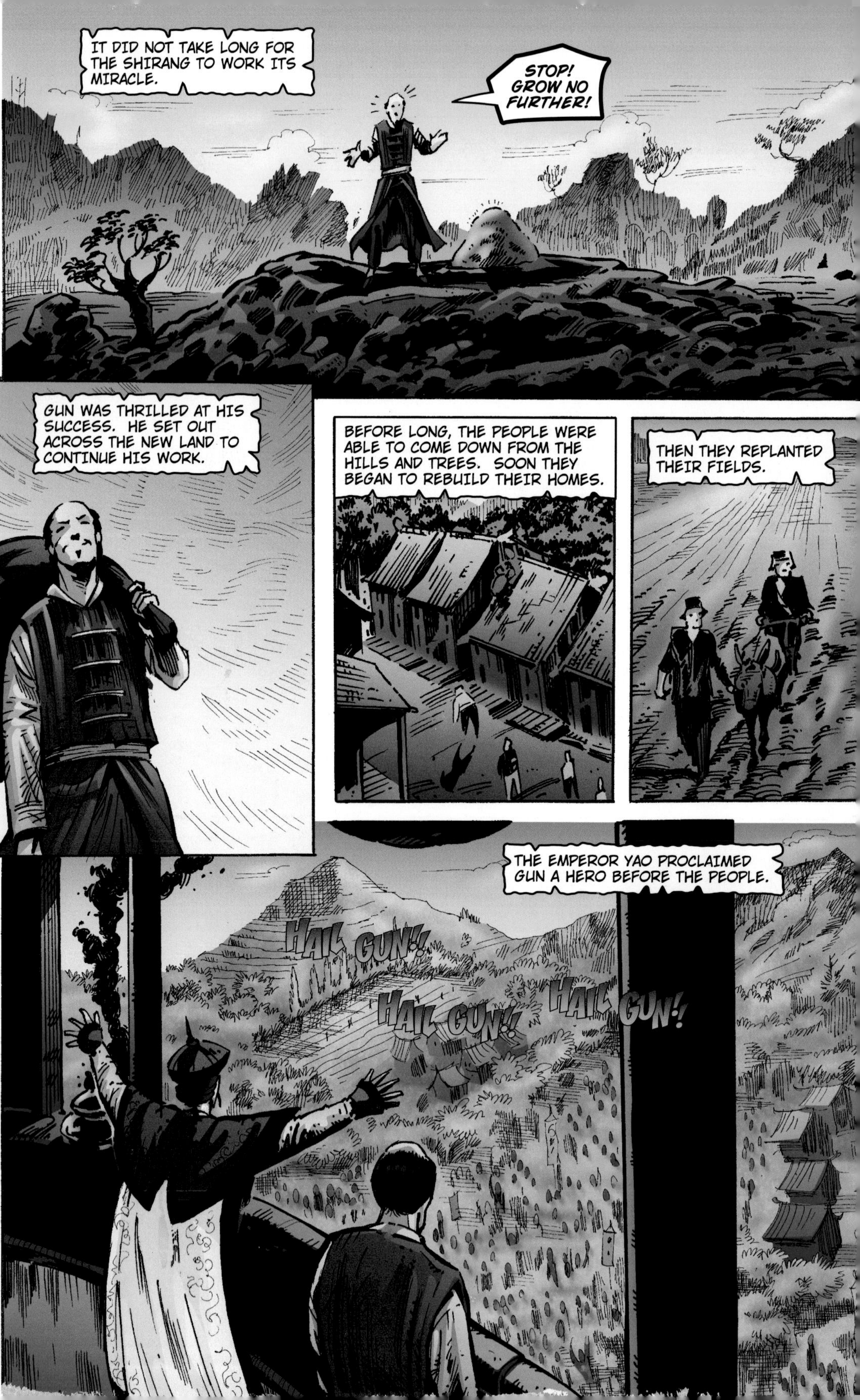
IT DID NOT TAKE LONG FOR THE SHIRANG TO WORK ITS MIRACLE.
STOP! GROW NO FURTHER!
GUN WAS THRILLED AT HIS SUCCESS. HE SET OUT ACROSS THE NEW LAND TO CONTINUE HIS WORK.
BEFORE LONG, THE PEOPLE WERE ABLE TO COME DOWN FROM THE HILLS AND TREES. SOON THEY BEGAN TO REBUILD THEIR HOMES.
THEN THEY REPLANTED THEIR FIELDS.
THE EMPEROR YAO PROCLAIMED GUN A HERO BEFORE THE PEOPLE.
HAIL GUN!!
HAIL GUN!!
HAIL GUN!!

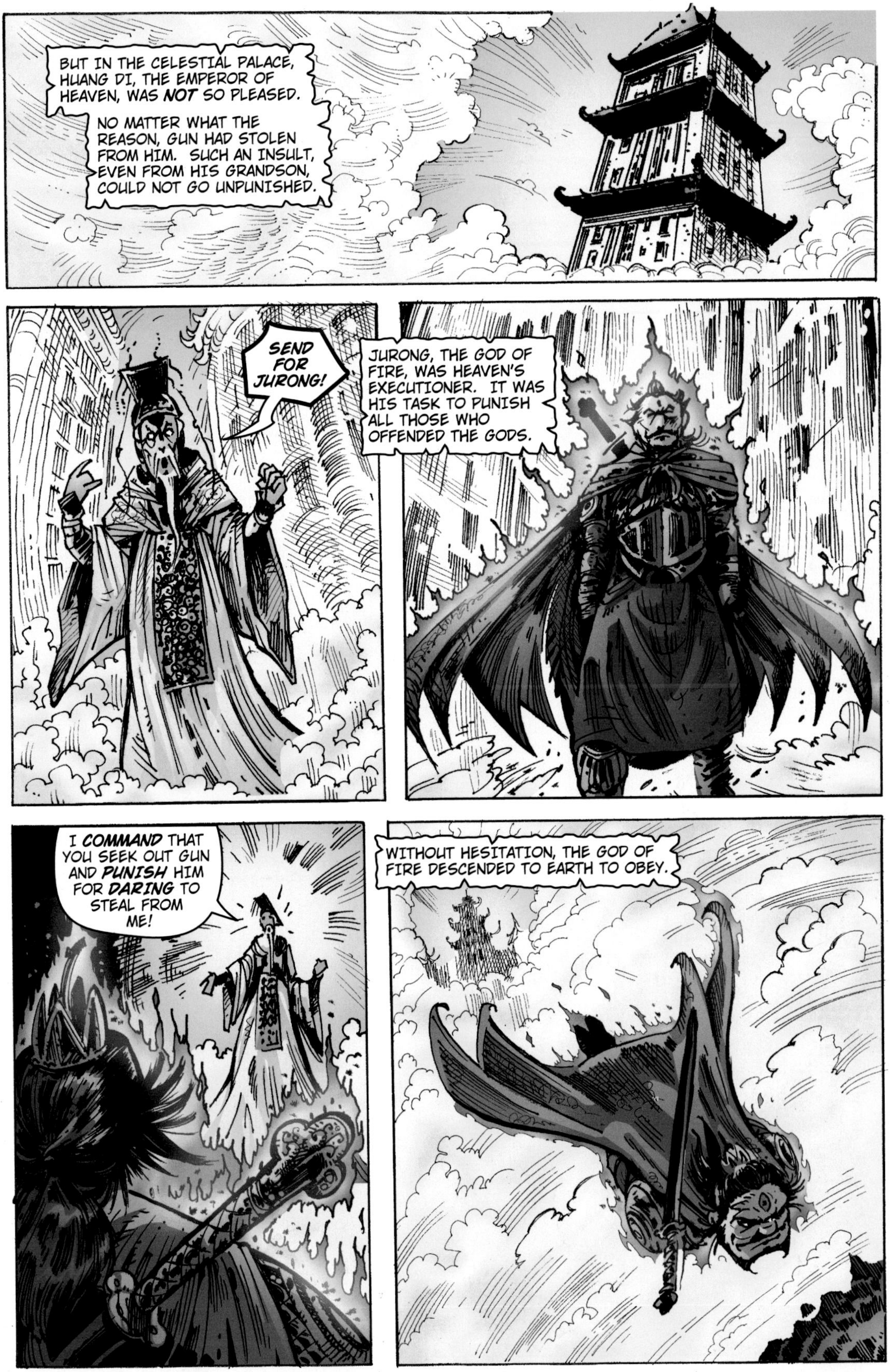
BUT IN THE CELESTIAL PALACE, HUANG DI, THE EMPEROR OF HEAVEN, WAS **NOT** SO PLEASED.
NO MATTER WHAT THE REASON, GUN HAD STOLEN FROM HIM. SUCH AN INSULT, EVEN FROM HIS GRANDSON, COULD NOT GO UNPUNISHED.
SEND FOR JURONG!
JURONG, THE GOD OF FIRE, WAS HEAVEN'S EXECUTIONER. IT WAS HIS TASK TO PUNISH ALL THOSE WHO OFFENDED THE GODS.
I **COMMAND** THAT YOU SEEK OUT GUN AND **PUNISH** HIM FOR **DARING** TO STEAL FROM ME!
WITHOUT HESITATION, THE GOD OF FIRE DESCENDED TO EARTH TO OBEY.

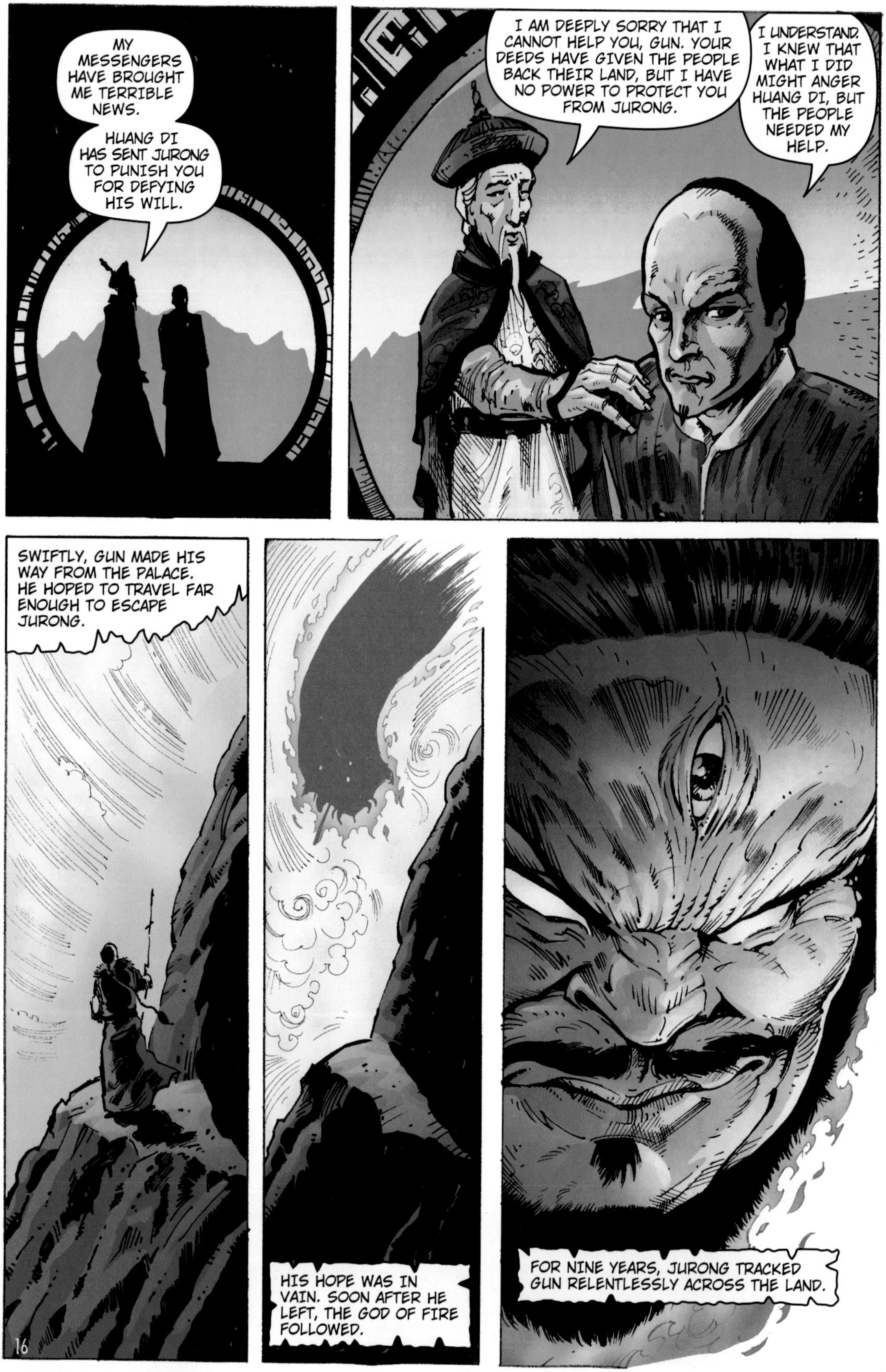
MY MESSENGERS HAVE BROUGHT ME TERRIBLE NEWS.
HUANG DI HAS SENT JURONG TO PUNISH YOU FOR DEFYING HIS WILL.
I AM DEEPLY SORRY THAT I CANNOT HELP YOU, GUN. YOUR DEEDS HAVE GIVEN THE PEOPLE BACK THEIR LAND, BUT I HAVE NO POWER TO PROTECT YOU FROM JURONG.
I UNDERSTAND. I KNEW THAT WHAT I DID MIGHT ANGER HUANG DI, BUT THE PEOPLE NEEDED MY HELP.
SWIFTLY, GUN MADE HIS WAY FROM THE PALACE. HE HOPED TO TRAVEL FAR ENOUGH TO ESCAPE JURONG.
HIS HOPE WAS IN VAIN. SOON AFTER HE LEFT, THE GOD OF FIRE FOLLOWED.
FOR NINE YEARS, JURONG TRACKED GUN RELENTLESSLY ACROSS THE LAND.

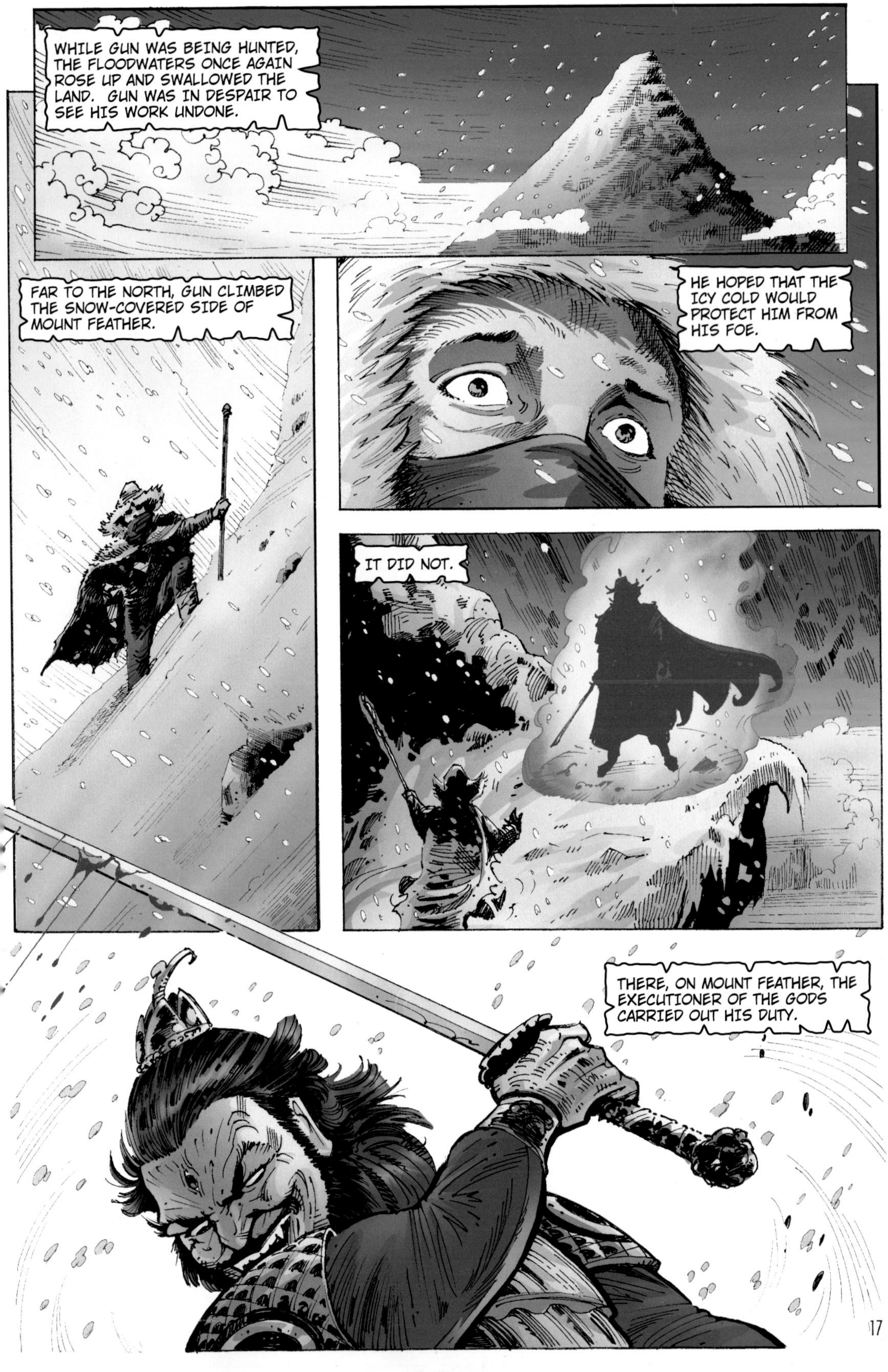
WHILE GUN WAS BEING HUNTED, THE FLOODWATERS ONCE AGAIN ROSE UP AND SWALLOWED THE LAND. GUN WAS IN DESPAIR TO SEE HIS WORK UNDONE.
FAR TO THE NORTH, GUN CLIMBED THE SNOW-COVERED SIDE OF MOUNT FEATHER.
HE HOPED THAT THE ICY COLD WOULD PROTECT HIM FROM HIS FOE.
IT DID NOT.
THERE, ON MOUNT FEATHER, THE EXECUTIONER OF THE GODS CARRIED OUT HIS DUTY.

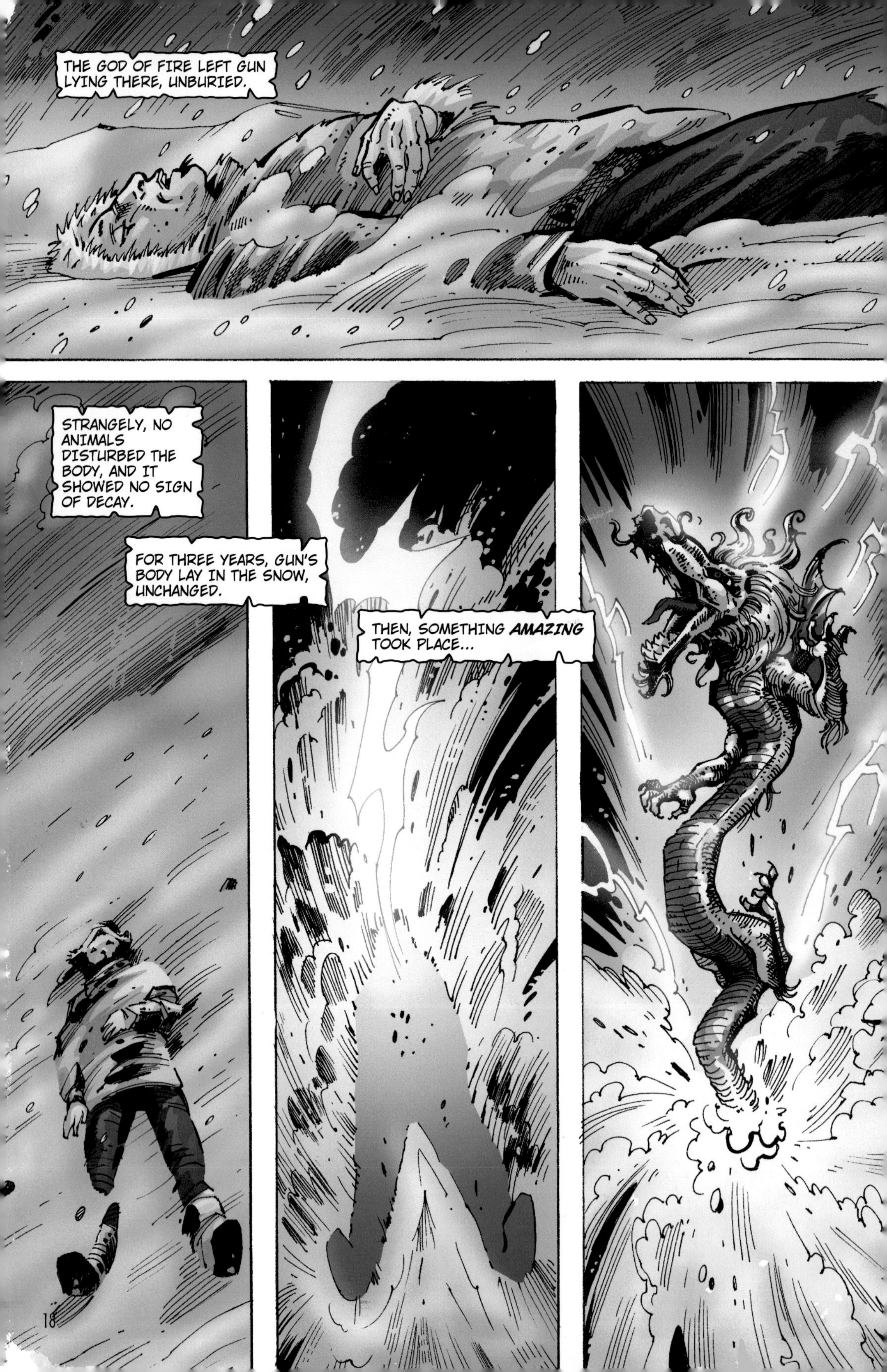
THE GOD OF FIRE LEFT GUN LYING THERE, UNBURIED.
STRANGELY, NO ANIMALS DISTURBED THE BODY, AND IT SHOWED NO SIGN OF DECAY.
FOR THREE YEARS, GUN'S BODY LAY IN THE SNOW, UNCHANGED.
THEN, SOMETHING *AMAZING* TOOK PLACE...

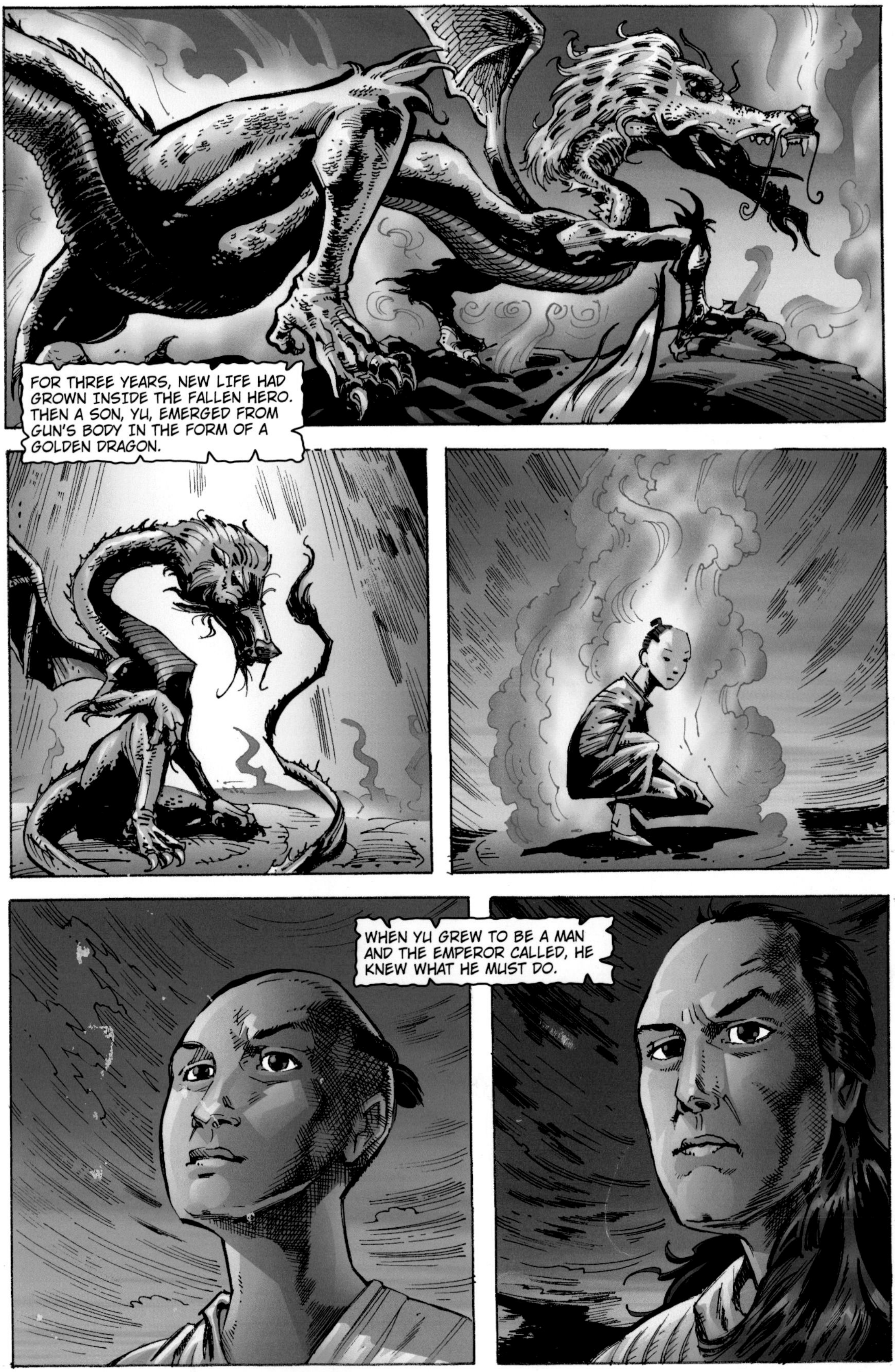
FOR THREE YEARS, NEW LIFE HAD GROWN INSIDE THE FALLEN HERO. THEN A SON, YU, EMERGED FROM GUN'S BODY IN THE FORM OF A GOLDEN DRAGON.
WHEN YU GREW TO BE A MAN AND THE EMPEROR CALLED, HE KNEW WHAT HE MUST DO.

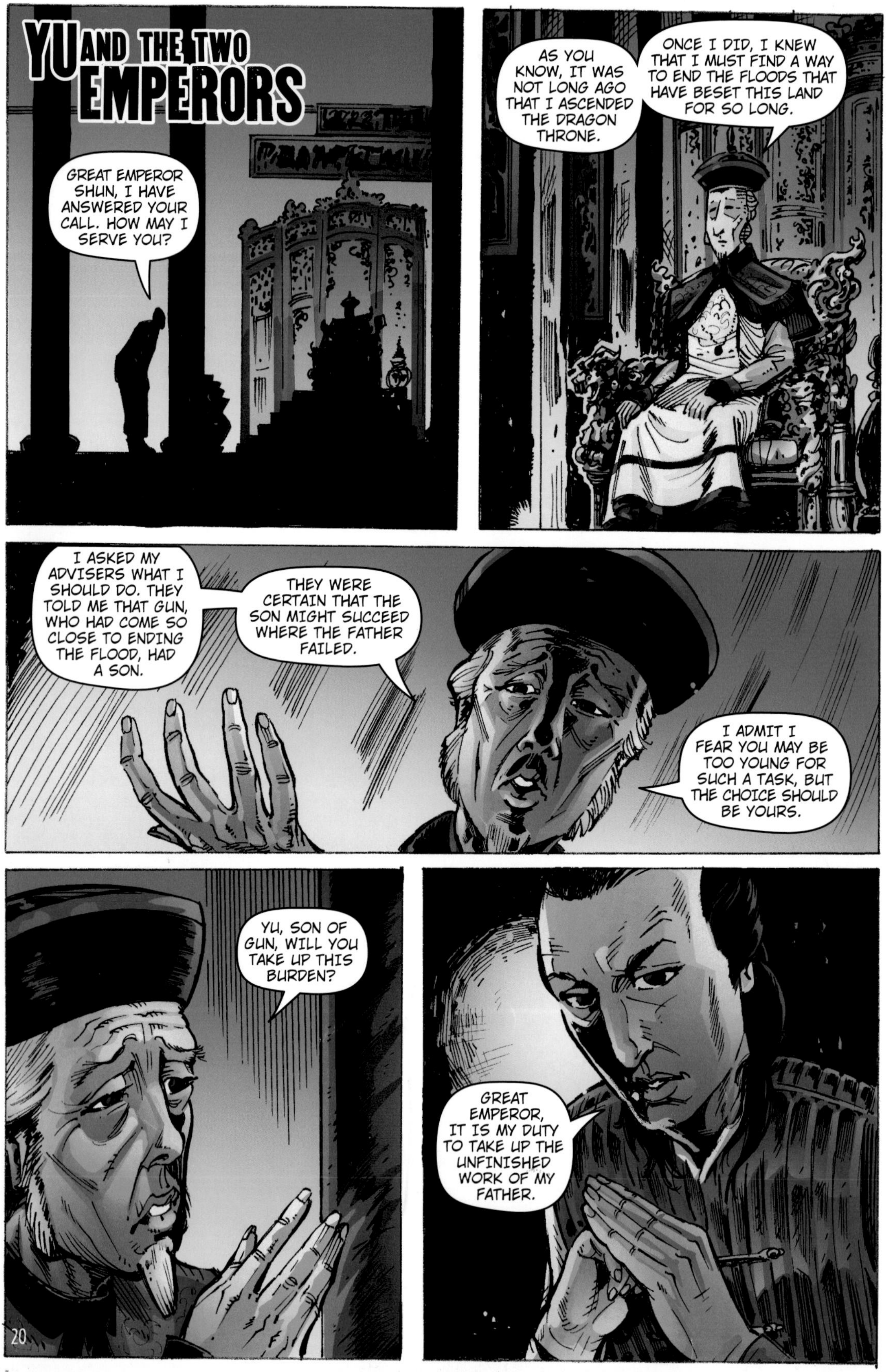
YU AND THE TWO EMPERORS
GREAT EMPEROR SHUN, I HAVE ANSWERED YOUR CALL. HOW MAY I SERVE YOU?
AS YOU KNOW, IT WAS NOT LONG AGO THAT I ASCENDED THE DRAGON THRONE.
ONCE I DID, I KNEW THAT I MUST FIND A WAY TO END THE FLOODS THAT HAVE BESET THIS LAND FOR SO LONG.
I ASKED MY ADVISERS WHAT I SHOULD DO. THEY TOLD ME THAT GUN, WHO HAD COME SO CLOSE TO ENDING THE FLOOD, HAD A SON.
THEY WERE CERTAIN THAT THE SON MIGHT SUCCEED WHERE THE FATHER FAILED.
I ADMIT I FEAR YOU MAY BE TOO YOUNG FOR SUCH A TASK, BUT THE CHOICE SHOULD BE YOURS.
YU, SON OF GUN, WILL YOU TAKE UP THIS BURDEN?
GREAT EMPEROR, IT IS MY DUTY TO TAKE UP THE UNFINISHED WORK OF MY FATHER.

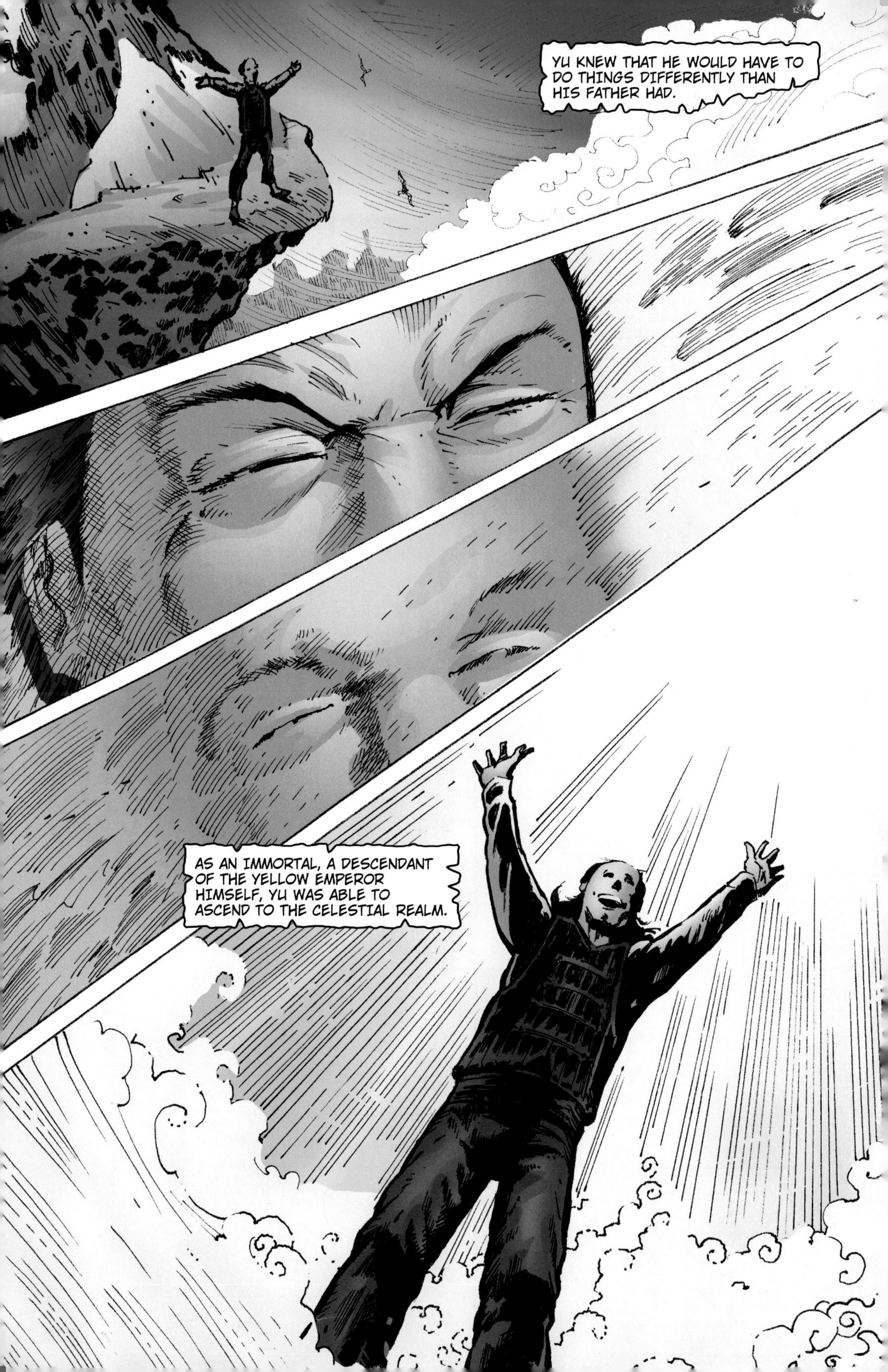
YU KNEW THAT HE WOULD HAVE TO DO THINGS DIFFERENTLY THAN HIS FATHER HAD.
AS AN IMMORTAL, A DESCENDANT OF THE YELLOW EMPEROR HIMSELF, YU WAS ABLE TO ASCEND TO THE CELESTIAL REALM.

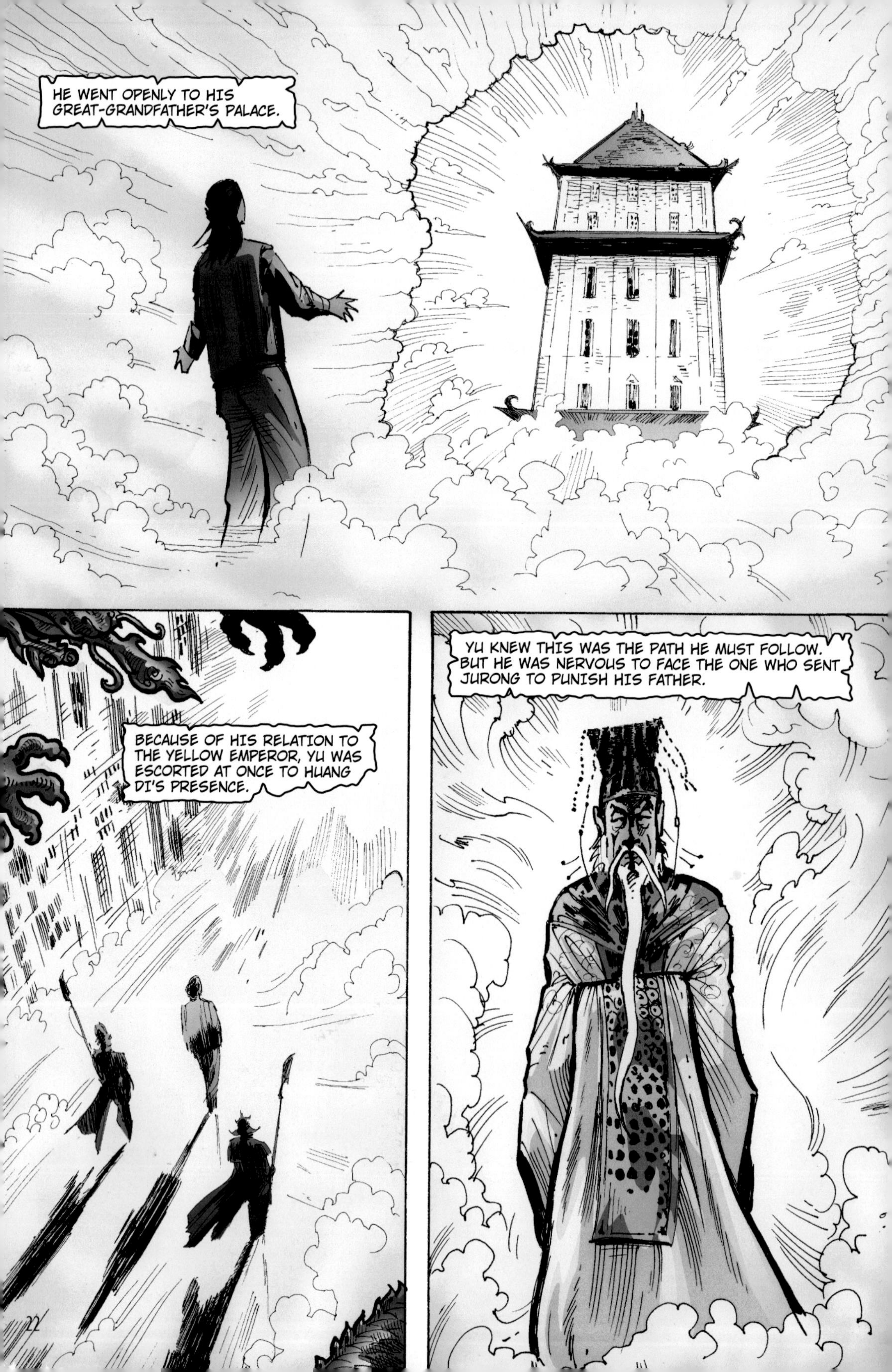
HE WENT OPENLY TO HIS GREAT-GRANDFATHER'S PALACE.
BECAUSE OF HIS RELATION TO THE YELLOW EMPEROR, YU WAS ESCORTED AT ONCE TO HUANG DI'S PRESENCE.
YU KNEW THIS WAS THE PATH HE MUST FOLLOW. BUT HE WAS NERVOUS TO FACE THE ONE WHO SENT JURONG TO PUNISH HIS FATHER.

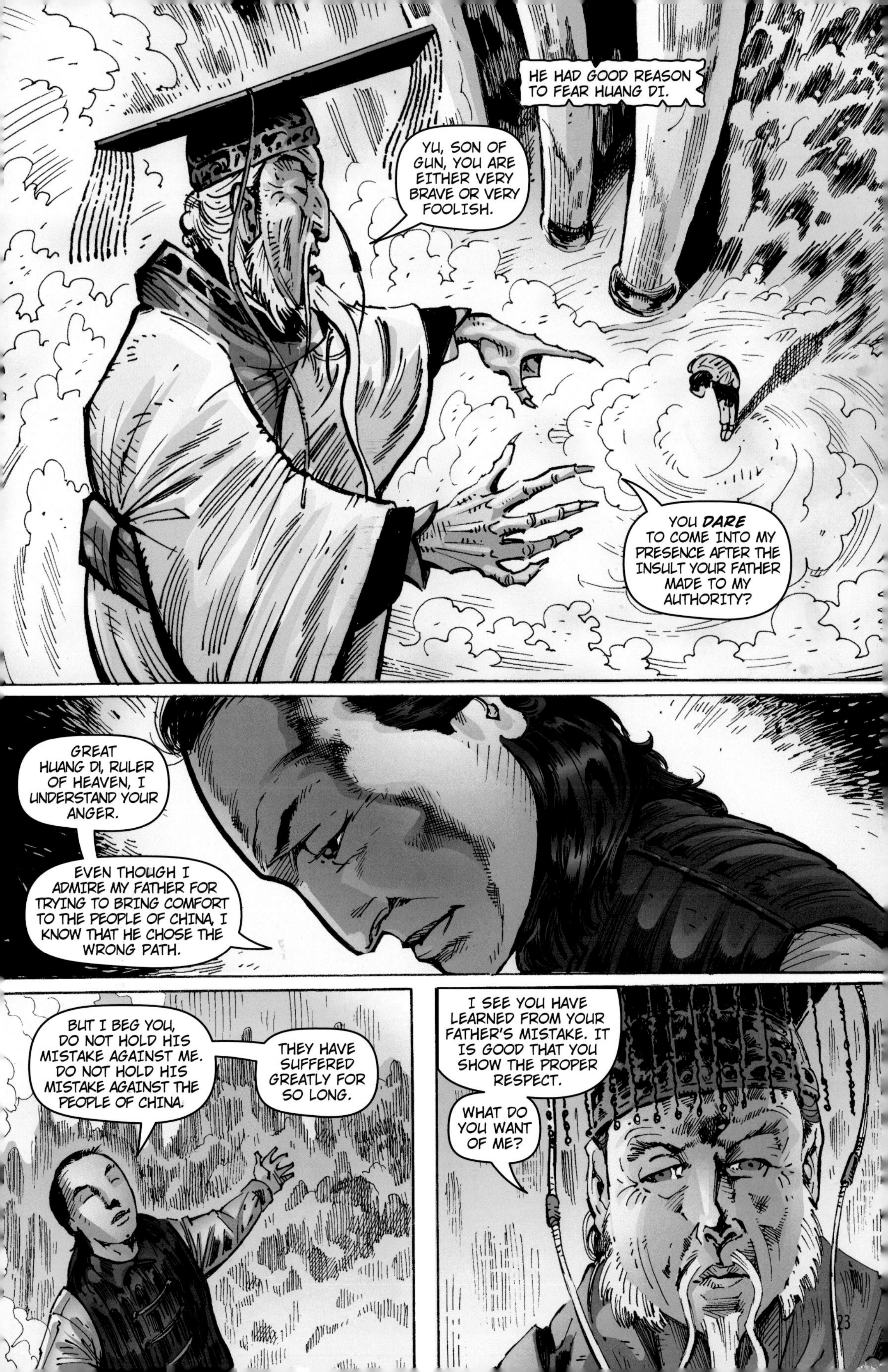
HE HAD GOOD REASON TO FEAR HUANG DI.
YU, SON OF GUN, YOU ARE EITHER VERY BRAVE OR VERY FOOLISH.
YOU DARE TO COME INTO MY PRESENCE AFTER THE INSULT YOUR FATHER MADE TO MY AUTHORITY?
GREAT HUANG DI, RULER OF HEAVEN, I UNDERSTAND YOUR ANGER.
EVEN THOUGH I ADMIRE MY FATHER FOR TRYING TO BRING COMFORT TO THE PEOPLE OF CHINA, I KNOW THAT HE CHOSE THE WRONG PATH.
BUT I BEG YOU, DO NOT HOLD HIS MISTAKE AGAINST ME. DO NOT HOLD HIS MISTAKE AGAINST THE PEOPLE OF CHINA.
THEY HAVE SUFFERED GREATLY FOR SO LONG.
I SEE YOU HAVE LEARNED FROM YOUR FATHER'S MISTAKE. IT IS GOOD THAT YOU SHOW THE PROPER RESPECT.
WHAT DO YOU WANT OF ME?

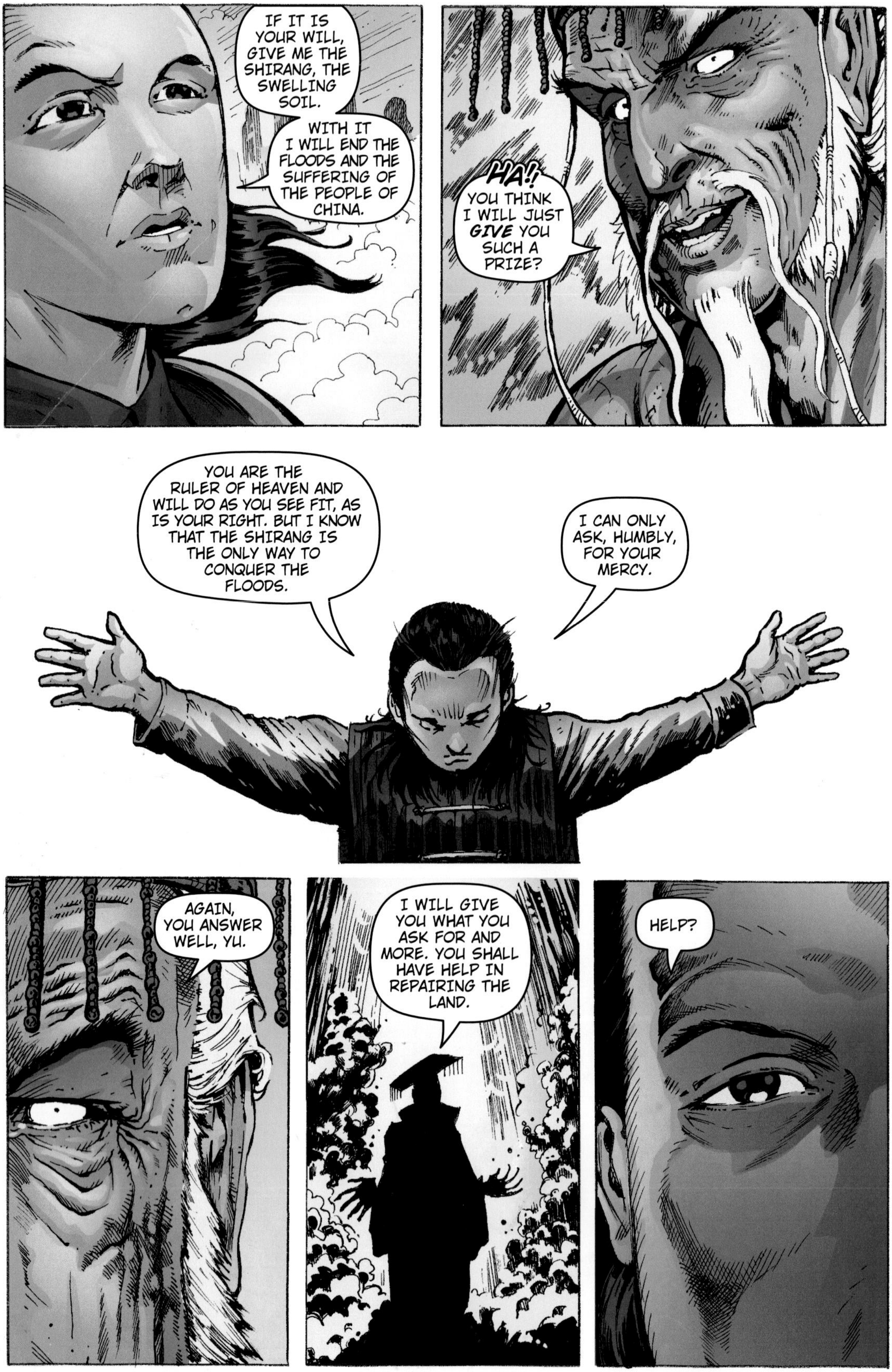
IF IT IS YOUR WILL, GIVE ME THE SHIRANG, THE SWELLING SOIL.
WITH IT I WILL END THE FLOODS AND THE SUFFERING OF THE PEOPLE OF CHINA.
HA!!
YOU THINK I WILL JUST GIVE YOU SUCH A PRIZE?
YOU ARE THE RULER OF HEAVEN AND WILL DO AS YOU SEE FIT, AS IS YOUR RIGHT. BUT I KNOW THAT THE SHIRANG IS THE ONLY WAY TO CONQUER THE FLOODS.
I CAN ONLY ASK, HUMBLY, FOR YOUR MERCY.
AGAIN, YOU ANSWER WELL, YU.
I WILL GIVE YOU WHAT YOU ASK FOR AND MORE. YOU SHALL HAVE HELP IN REPAIRING THE LAND.
HELP?

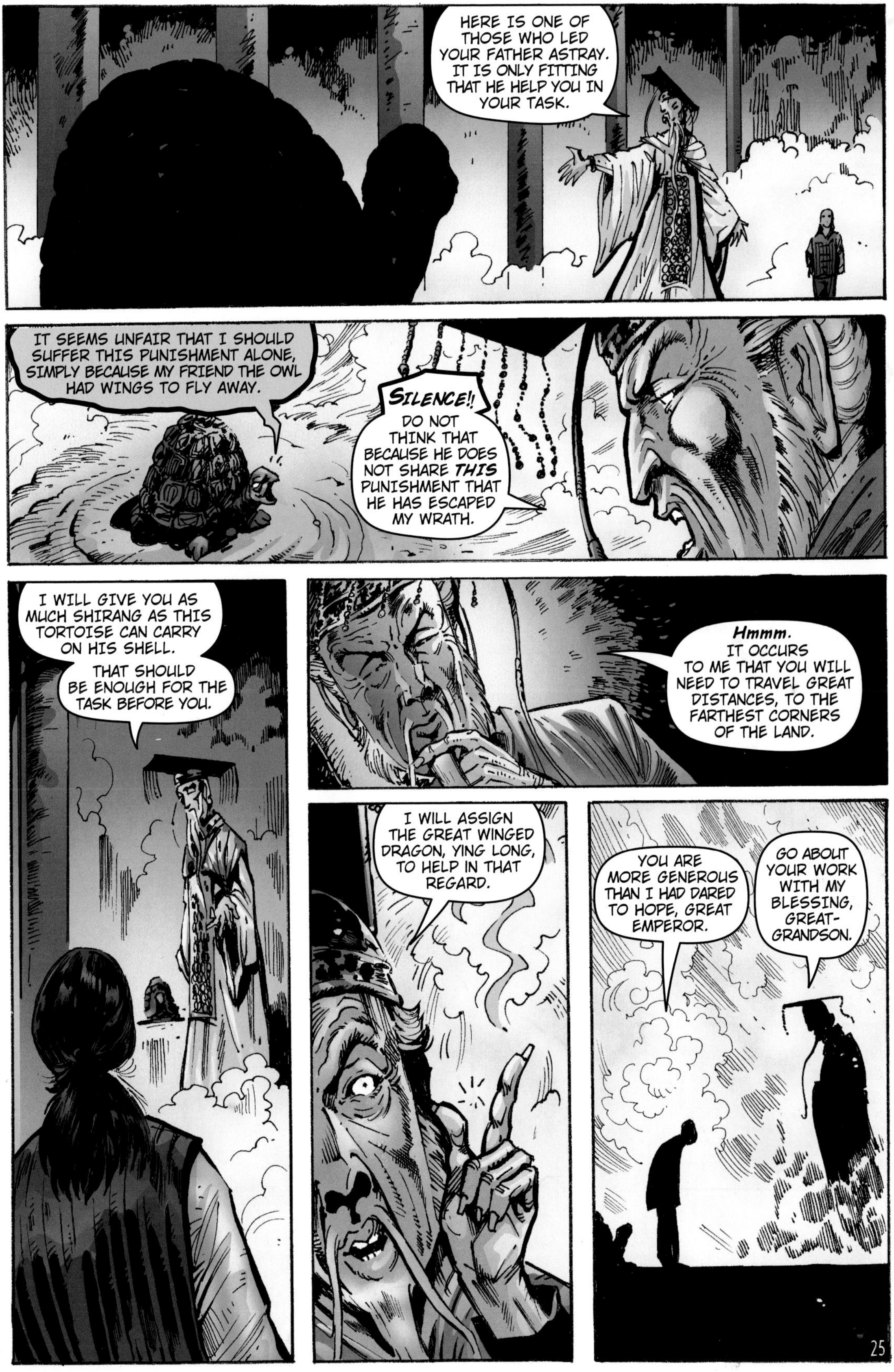
HERE IS ONE OF THOSE WHO LED YOUR FATHER ASTRAY. IT IS ONLY FITTING THAT HE HELP YOU IN YOUR TASK.
IT SEEMS UNFAIR THAT I SHOULD SUFFER THIS PUNISHMENT ALONE, SIMPLY BECAUSE MY FRIEND THE OWL HAD WINGS TO FLY AWAY.
SILENCE!! DO NOT THINK THAT BECAUSE HE DOES NOT SHARE THIS PUNISHMENT THAT HE HAS ESCAPED MY WRATH.
I WILL GIVE YOU AS MUCH SHIRANG AS THIS TORTOISE CAN CARRY ON HIS SHELL.
THAT SHOULD BE ENOUGH FOR THE TASK BEFORE YOU.
Hmmm. IT OCCURS TO ME THAT YOU WILL NEED TO TRAVEL GREAT DISTANCES, TO THE FARTHEST CORNERS OF THE LAND.
I WILL ASSIGN THE GREAT WINGED DRAGON, YING LONG, TO HELP IN THAT REGARD.
YOU ARE MORE GENEROUS THAN I HAD DARED TO HOPE, GREAT EMPEROR.
GO ABOUT YOUR WORK WITH MY BLESSING, GREAT-GRANDSON.

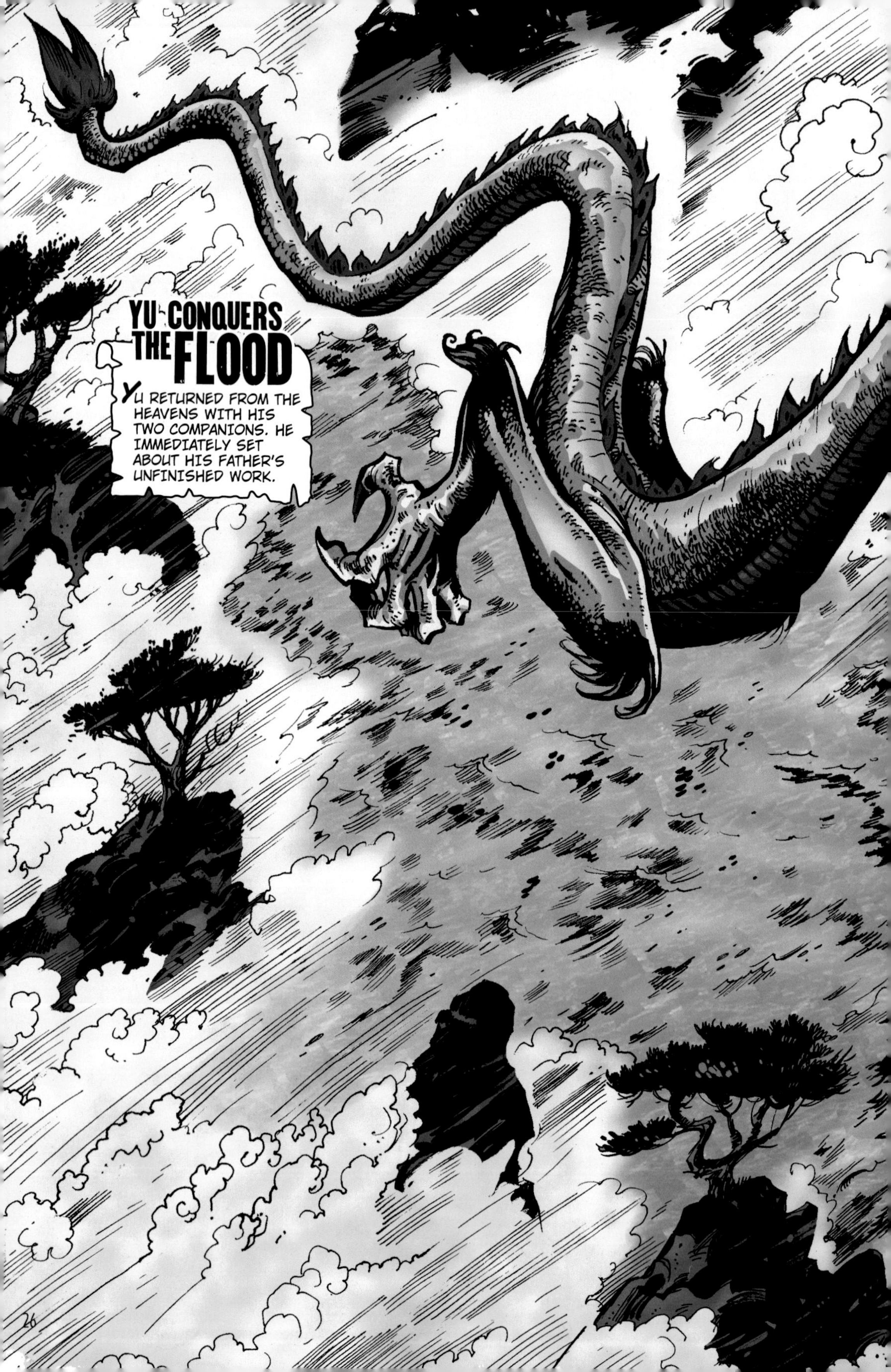
YU CONQUERS THE FLOOD
YU RETURNED FROM THE HEAVENS WITH HIS TWO COMPANIONS. HE IMMEDIATELY SET ABOUT HIS FATHER'S UNFINISHED WORK.

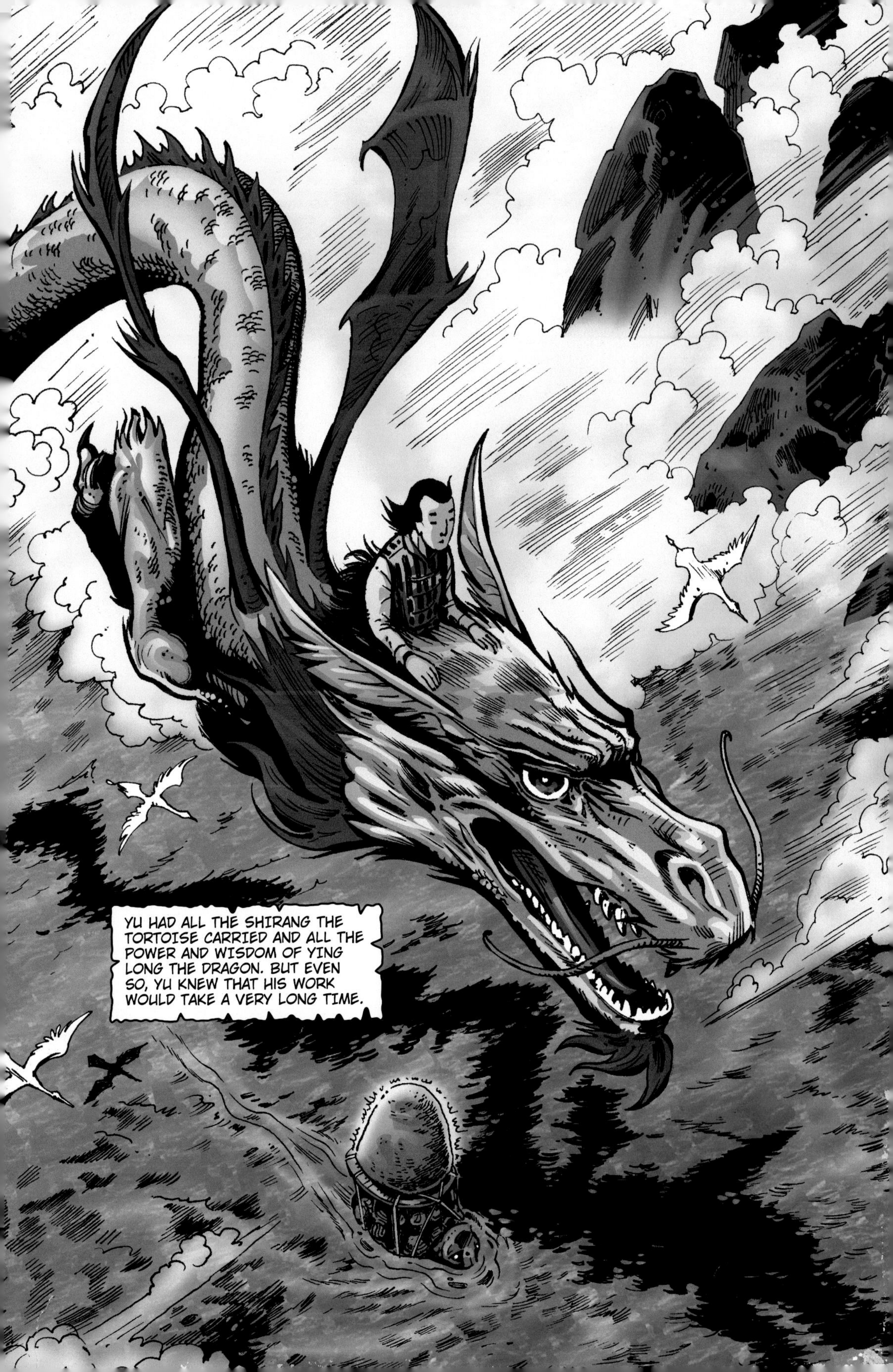
YU HAD ALL THE SHIRANG THE TORTOISE CARRIED AND ALL THE POWER AND WISDOM OF YING LONG THE DRAGON. BUT EVEN SO, YU KNEW THAT HIS WORK WOULD TAKE A VERY LONG TIME.

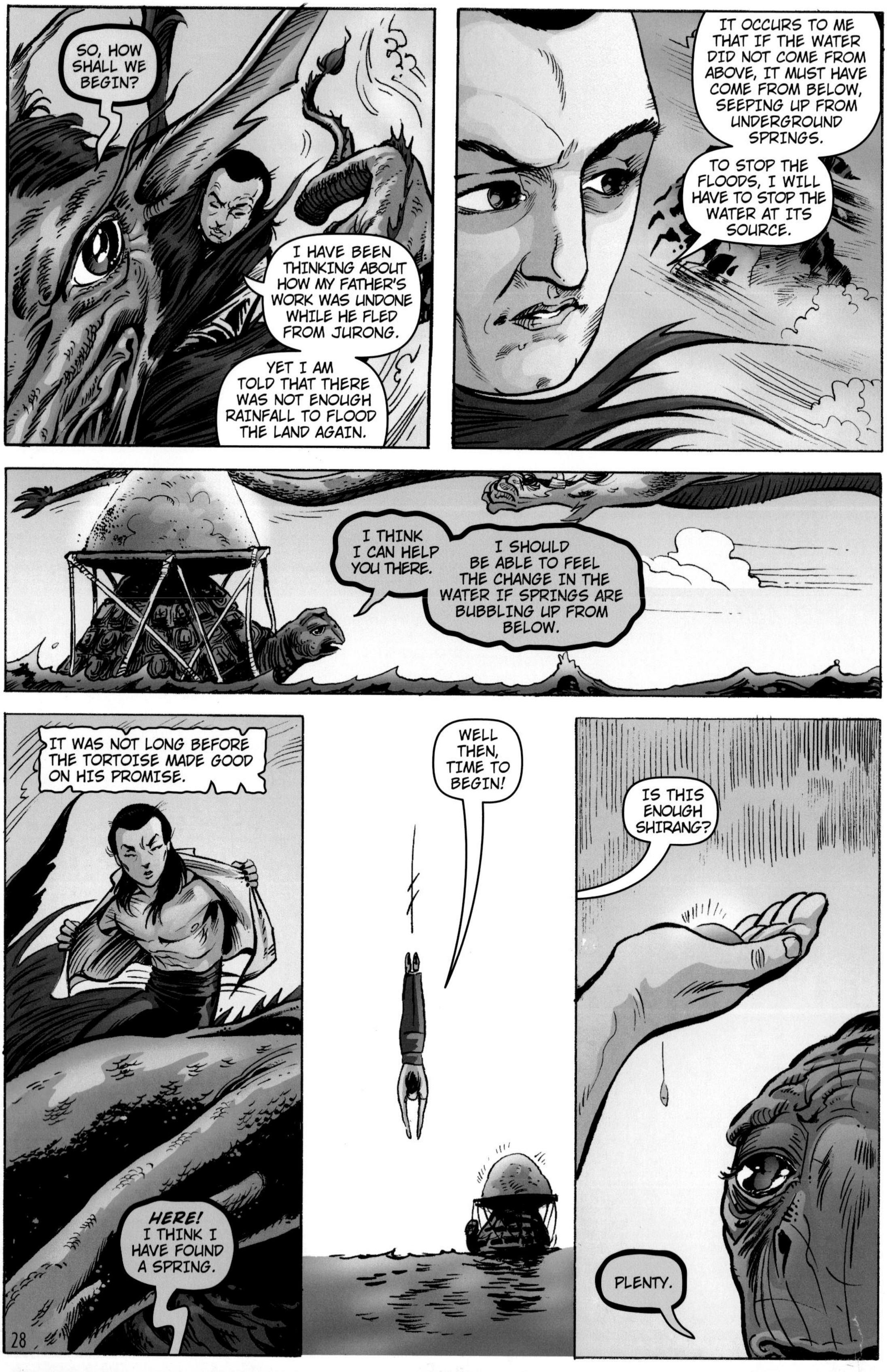
SO, HOW SHALL WE BEGIN?
I HAVE BEEN THINKING ABOUT HOW MY FATHER'S WORK WAS UNDONE WHILE HE FLED FROM JURONG.
YET I AM TOLD THAT THERE WAS NOT ENOUGH RAINFALL TO FLOOD THE LAND AGAIN.
IT OCCURS TO ME THAT IF THE WATER DID NOT COME FROM ABOVE, IT MUST HAVE COME FROM BELOW, SEEPING UP FROM UNDERGROUND SPRINGS.
TO STOP THE FLOODS, I WILL HAVE TO STOP THE WATER AT ITS SOURCE.
I THINK I CAN HELP YOU THERE.
I SHOULD BE ABLE TO FEEL THE CHANGE IN THE WATER IF SPRINGS ARE BUBBLING UP FROM BELOW.
IT WAS NOT LONG BEFORE THE TORTOISE MADE GOOD ON HIS PROMISE.
HERE! I THINK I HAVE FOUND A SPRING.
WELL THEN, TIME TO BEGIN!
IS THIS ENOUGH SHIRANG?
PLENTY.

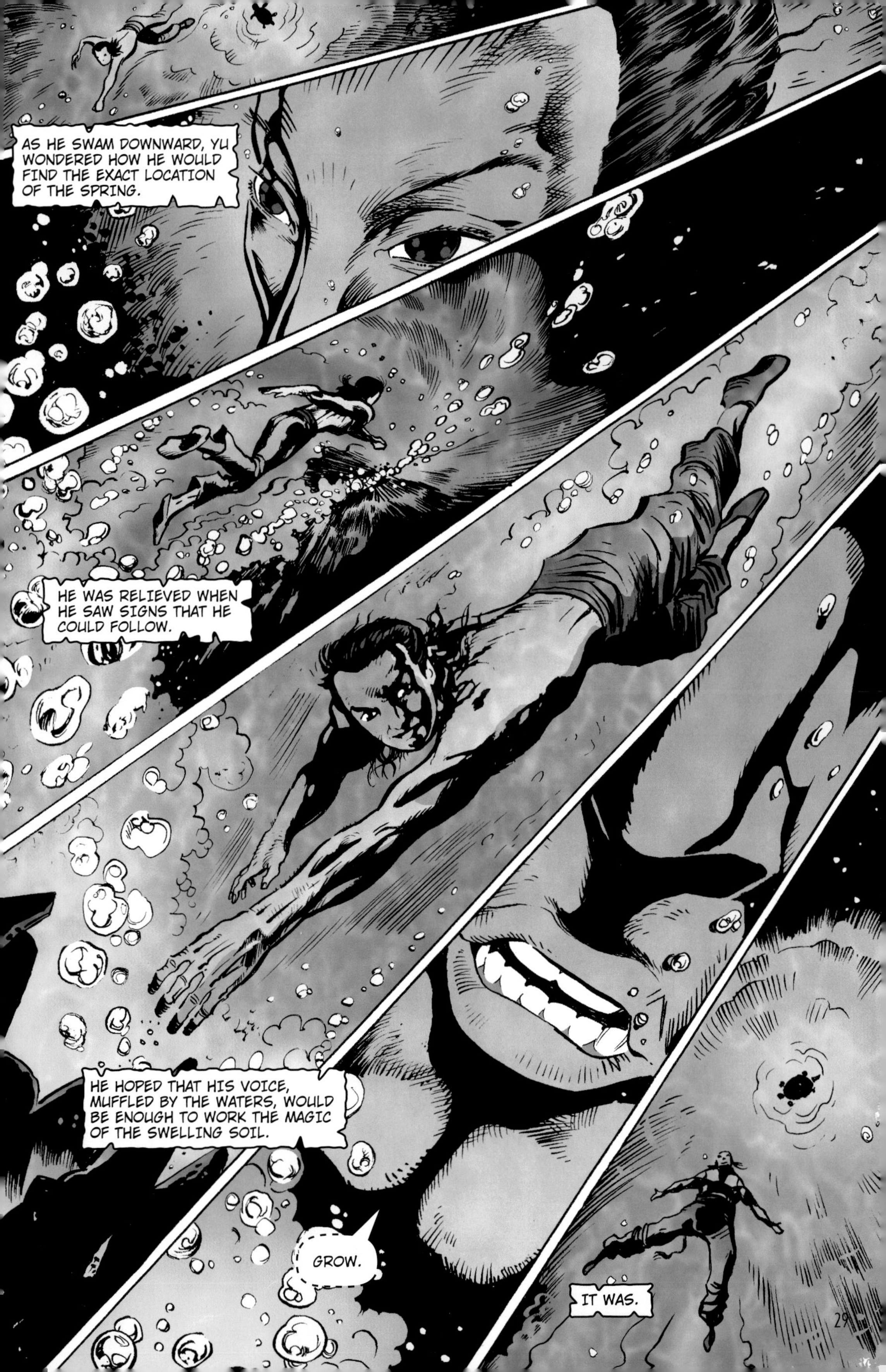
AS HE SWAM DOWNWARD, YU WONDERED HOW HE WOULD FIND THE EXACT LOCATION OF THE SPRING.
HE WAS RELIEVED WHEN HE SAW SIGNS THAT HE COULD FOLLOW.
HE HOPED THAT HIS VOICE, MUFFLED BY THE WATERS, WOULD BE ENOUGH TO WORK THE MAGIC OF THE SWELLING SOIL.
GROW.
IT WAS.

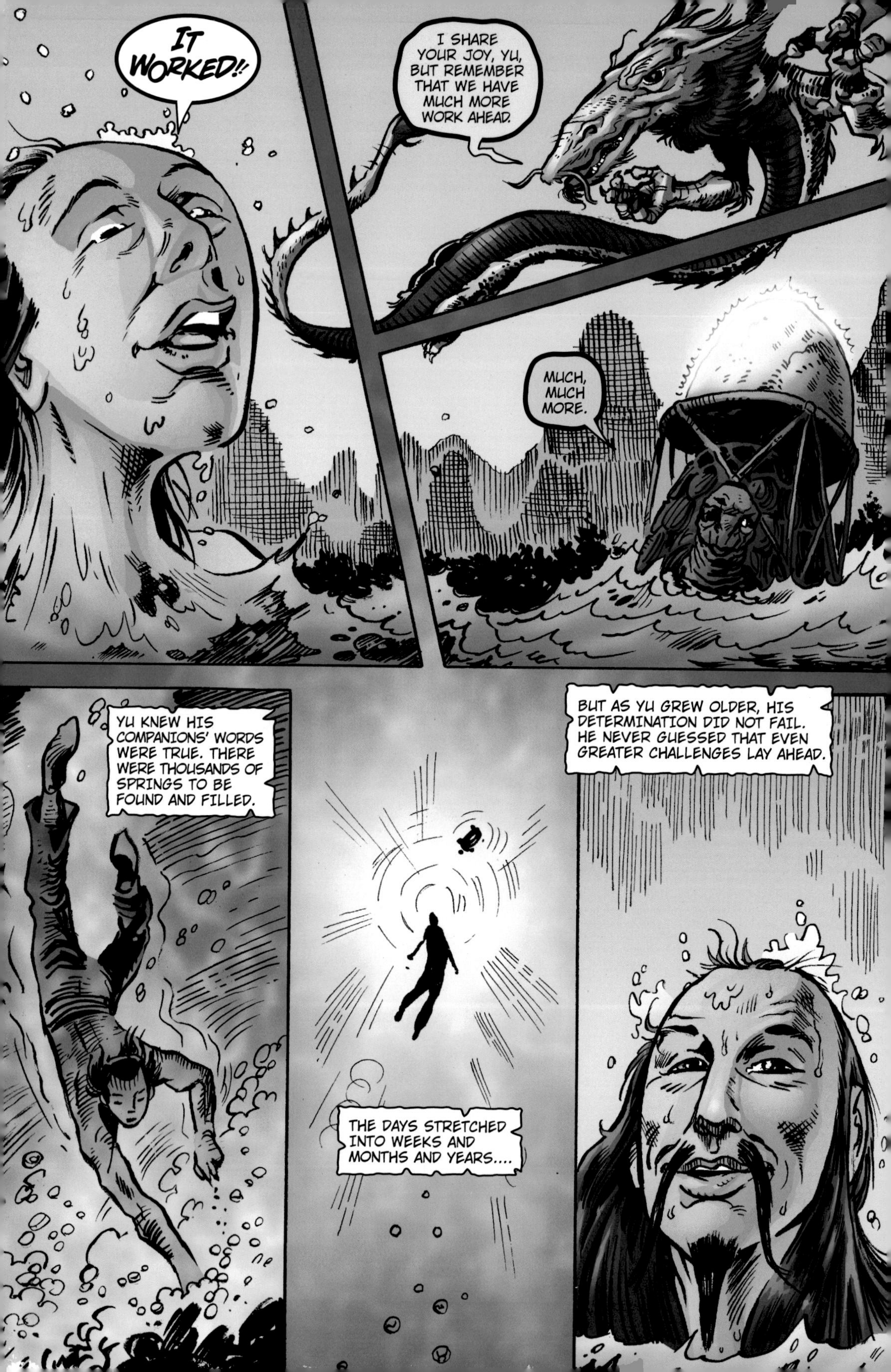
IT WORKED!!
I SHARE YOUR JOY, YU, BUT REMEMBER THAT WE HAVE MUCH MORE WORK AHEAD.
MUCH, MUCH MORE.
YU KNEW HIS COMPANIONS' WORDS WERE TRUE. THERE WERE THOUSANDS OF SPRINGS TO BE FOUND AND FILLED.
THE DAYS STRETCHED INTO WEEKS AND MONTHS AND YEARS....
BUT AS YU GREW OLDER, HIS DETERMINATION DID NOT FAIL. HE NEVER GUESSED THAT EVEN GREATER CHALLENGES LAY AHEAD.

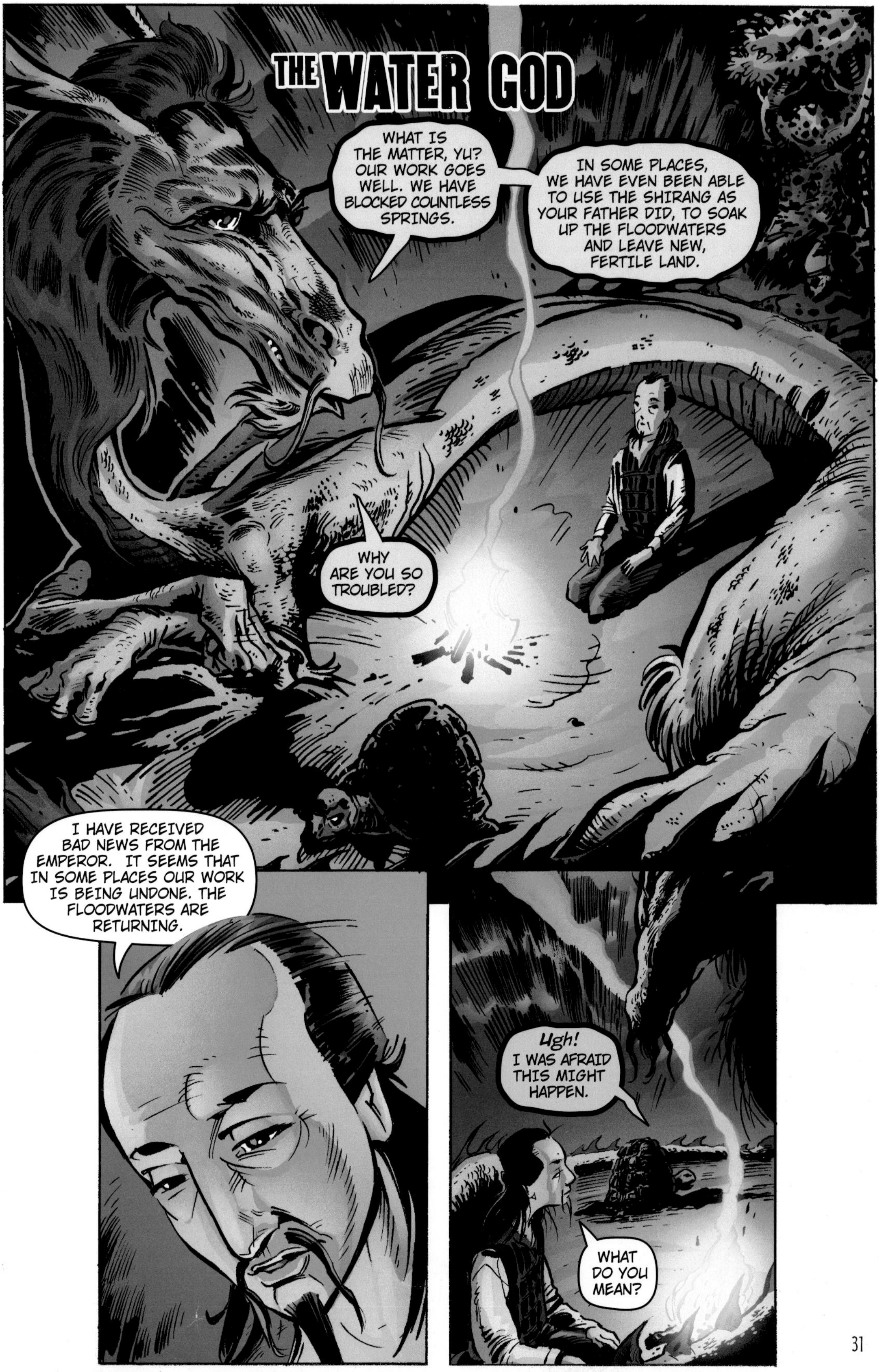
THE WATER GOD
WHAT IS THE MATTER, YU? OUR WORK GOES WELL. WE HAVE BLOCKED COUNTLESS SPRINGS.
IN SOME PLACES, WE HAVE EVEN BEEN ABLE TO USE THE SHIRANG AS YOUR FATHER DID, TO SOAK UP THE FLOODWATERS AND LEAVE NEW, FERTILE LAND.
WHY ARE YOU SO TROUBLED?
I HAVE RECEIVED BAD NEWS FROM THE EMPEROR. IT SEEMS THAT IN SOME PLACES OUR WORK IS BEING UNDONE. THE FLOODWATERS ARE RETURNING.
Ugh! I WAS AFRAID THIS MIGHT HAPPEN.
WHAT DO YOU MEAN?

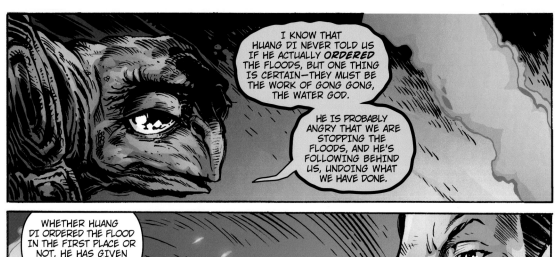

I KNOW THAT HUANG DI NEVER TOLD US IF HE ACTUALLY *ORDERED* THE FLOODS, BUT ONE THING IS CERTAIN—THEY MUST BE THE WORK OF GONG GONG, THE WATER GOD.

HE IS PROBABLY ANGRY THAT WE ARE STOPPING THE FLOODS, AND HE'S FOLLOWING BEHIND US, UNDOING WHAT WE HAVE DONE.

WHETHER HUANG DI ORDERED THE FLOOD IN THE FIRST PLACE OR NOT, HE HAS GIVEN HIS BLESSING TO OUR WORK.

WHY WOULD HE LET GONG GONG INTERFERE?

PERHAPS HUANG DI WANTS US TO DEAL WITH GONG GONG AS PART OF OUR WORK.

EVEN WITH YOUR HELP, YING LONG...

Ahem.

AND YOURS TOO, TORTOISE...

I FEAR THAT GONG GONG IS TOO POWERFUL TO DEFEAT.

I THINK THAT IN THE MORNING, WE WILL HAVE TO LOOK FOR OTHER ALLIES!

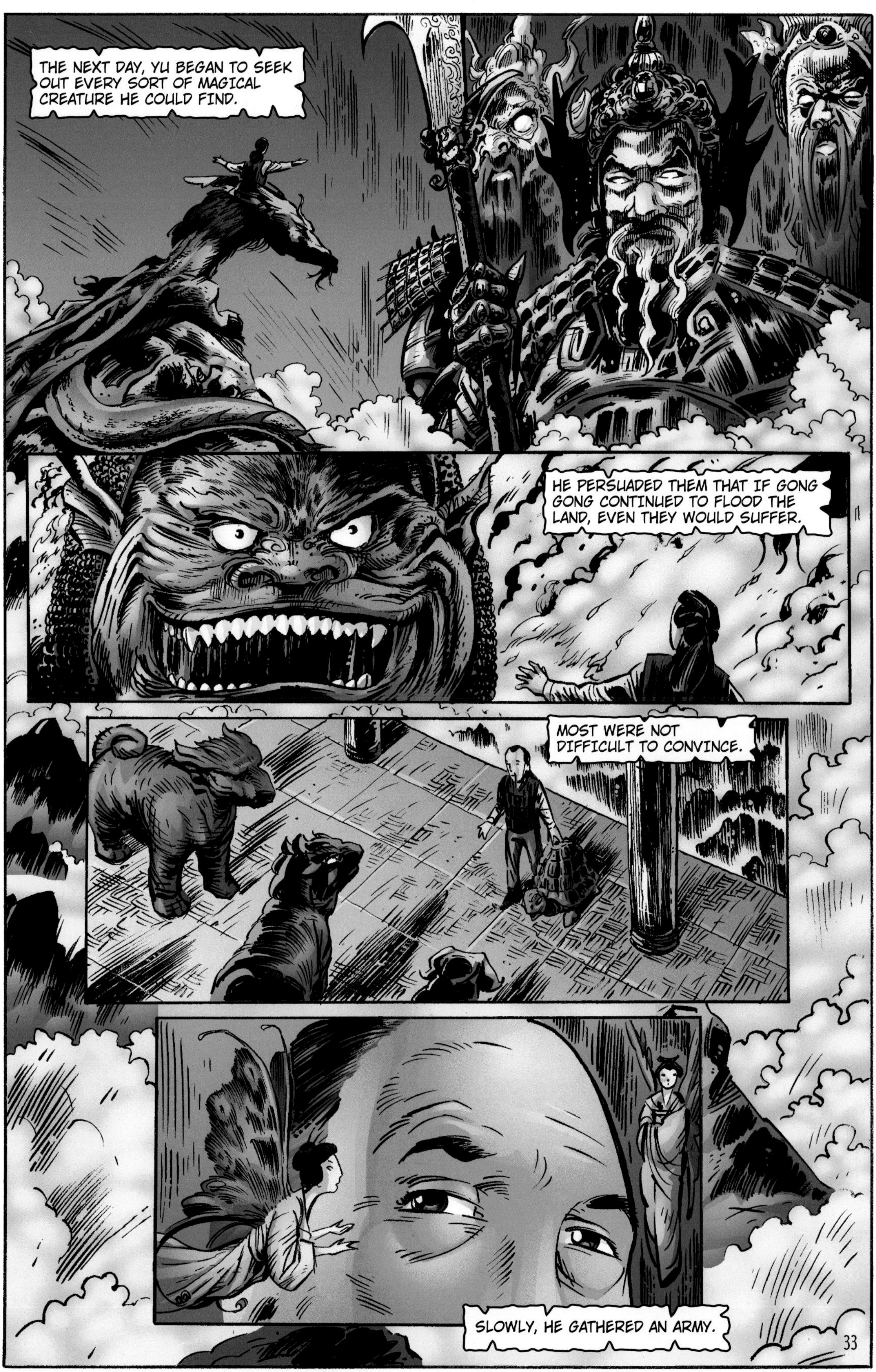
THE NEXT DAY, YU BEGAN TO SEEK OUT EVERY SORT OF MAGICAL CREATURE HE COULD FIND.
HE PERSUADED THEM THAT IF GONG GONG CONTINUED TO FLOOD THE LAND, EVEN THEY WOULD SUFFER.
MOST WERE NOT DIFFICULT TO CONVINCE.
SLOWLY, HE GATHERED AN ARMY.

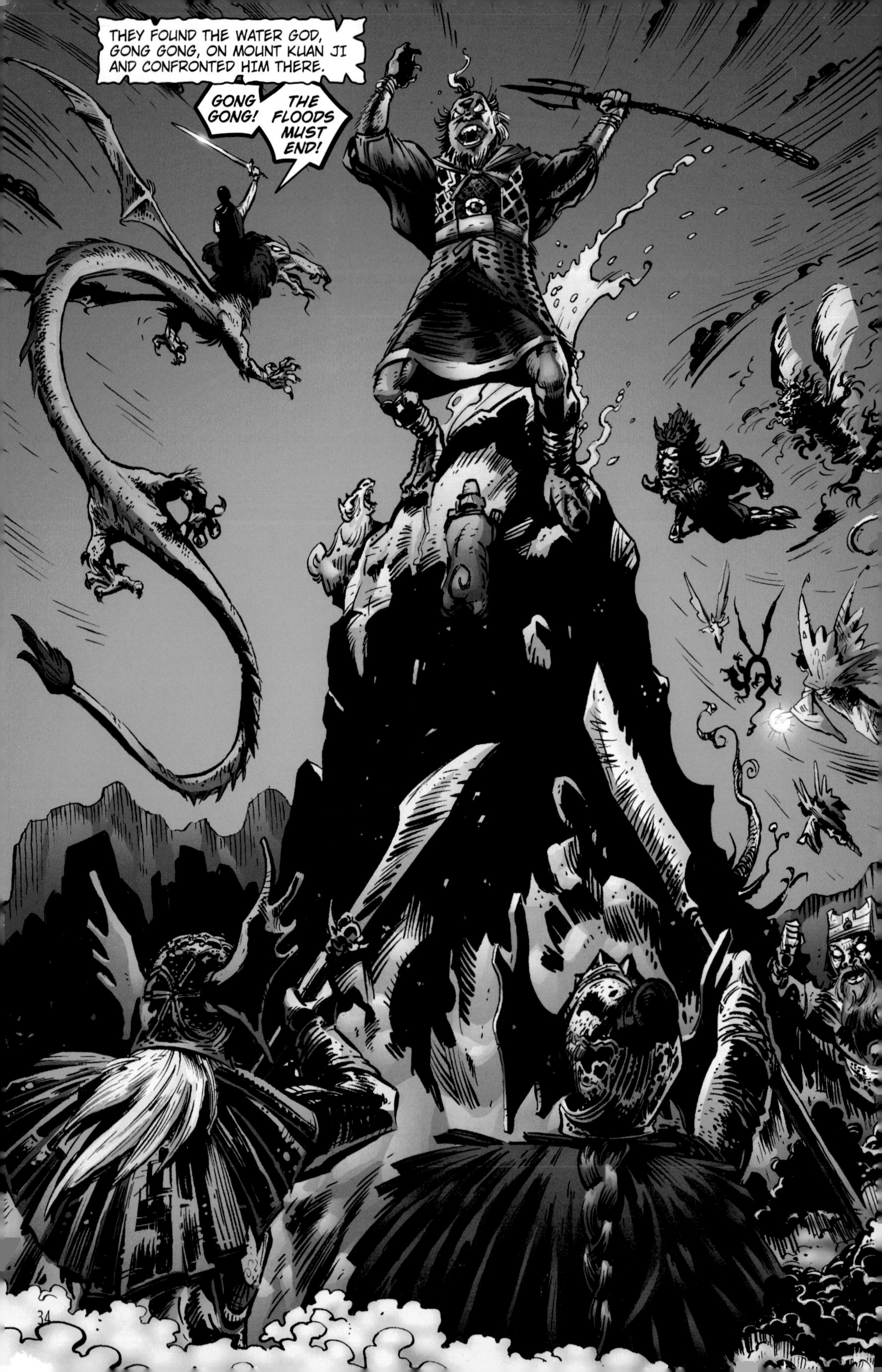
THEY FOUND THE WATER GOD, GONG GONG, ON MOUNT KUAN JI AND CONFRONTED HIM THERE.
GONG GONG!
THE FLOODS MUST END!

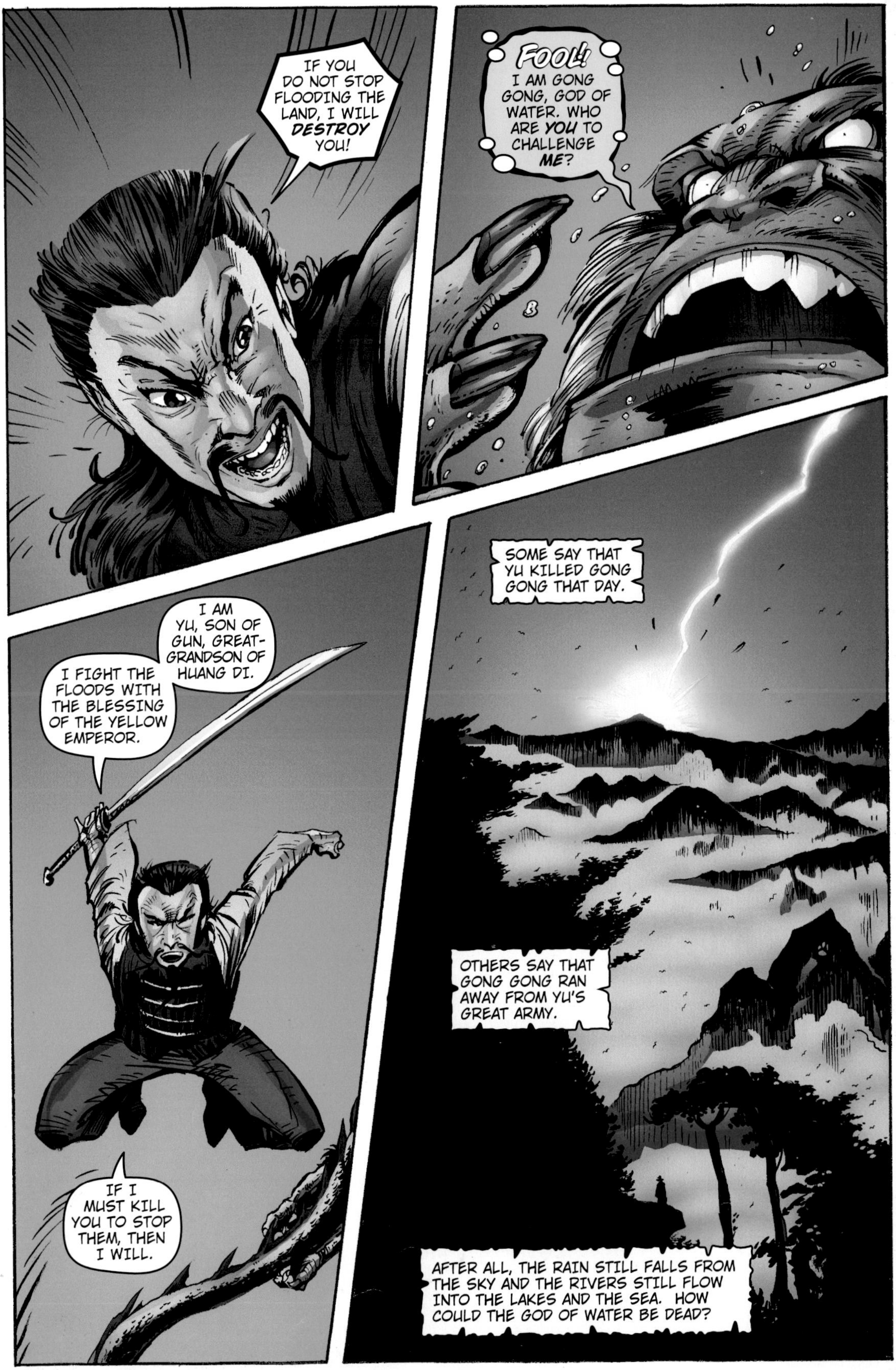
IF YOU DO NOT STOP FLOODING THE LAND, I WILL DESTROY YOU!
FOOL! I AM GONG GONG, GOD OF WATER. WHO ARE YOU TO CHALLENGE ME?
I AM YU, SON OF GUN, GREAT-GRANDSON OF HUANG DI.
I FIGHT THE FLOODS WITH THE BLESSING OF THE YELLOW EMPEROR.
IF I MUST KILL YOU TO STOP THEM, THEN I WILL.
SOME SAY THAT YU KILLED GONG GONG THAT DAY.
OTHERS SAY THAT GONG GONG RAN AWAY FROM YU'S GREAT ARMY.
AFTER ALL, THE RAIN STILL FALLS FROM THE SKY AND THE RIVERS STILL FLOW INTO THE LAKES AND THE SEA. HOW COULD THE GOD OF WATER BE DEAD?

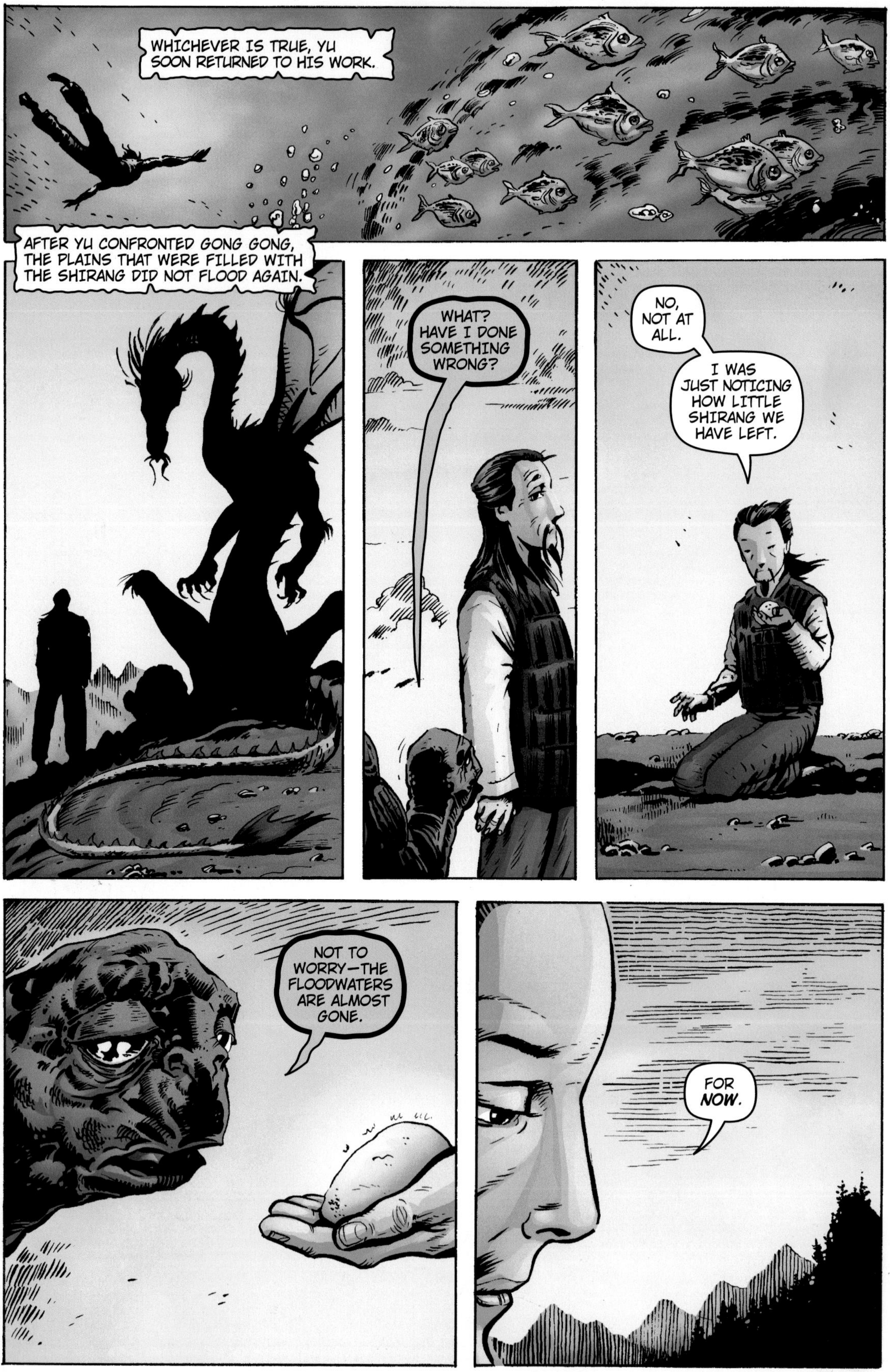
WHICHEVER IS TRUE, YU SOON RETURNED TO HIS WORK.
AFTER YU CONFRONTED GONG GONG, THE PLAINS THAT WERE FILLED WITH THE SHIRANG DID NOT FLOOD AGAIN.
WHAT? HAVE I DONE SOMETHING WRONG?
NO, NOT AT ALL.
I WAS JUST NOTICING HOW LITTLE SHIRANG WE HAVE LEFT.
NOT TO WORRY—THE FLOODWATERS ARE ALMOST GONE.
FOR *NOW*.

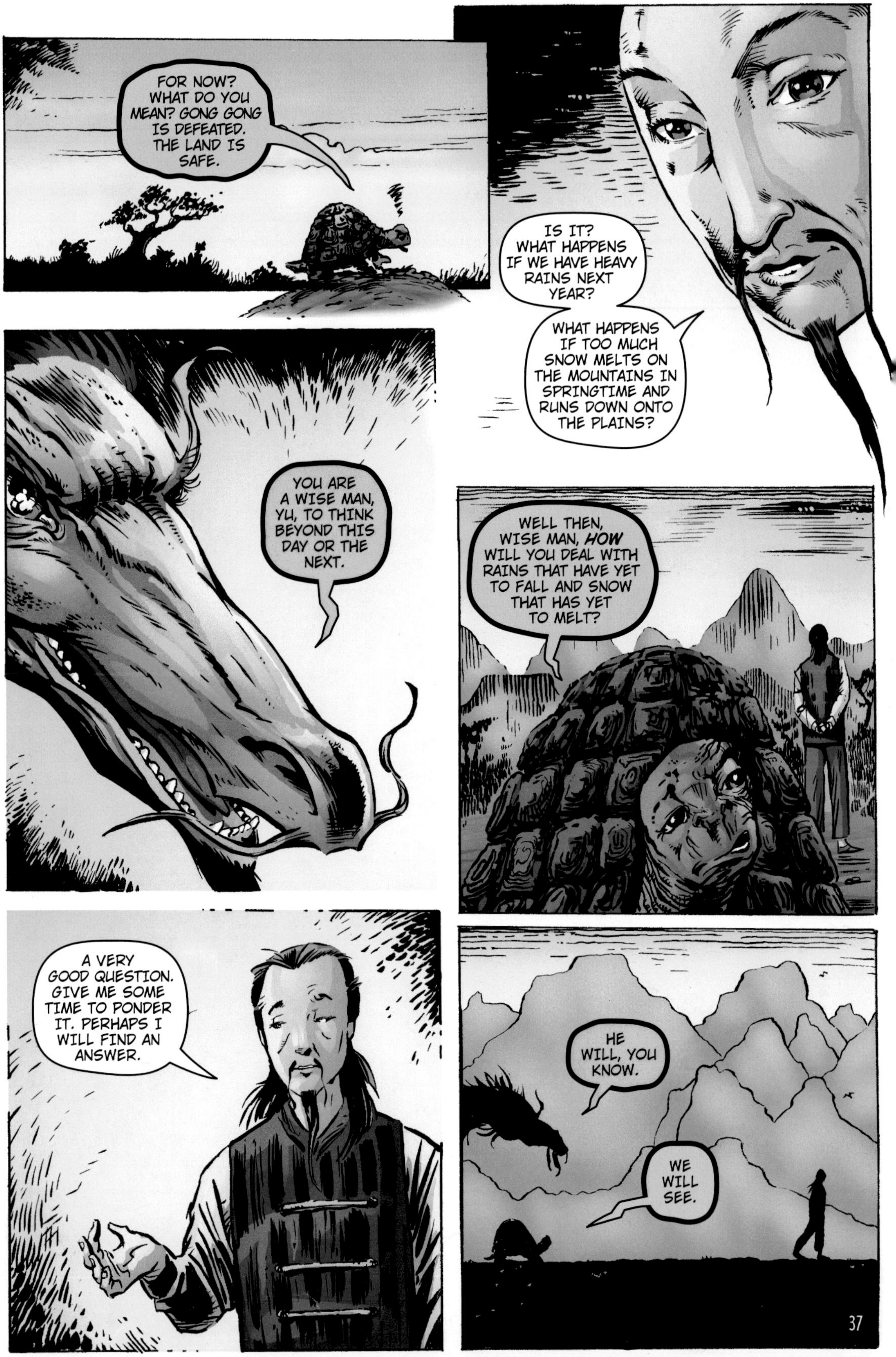

FOR NOW? WHAT DO YOU MEAN? GONG GONG IS DEFEATED. THE LAND IS SAFE.
IS IT? WHAT HAPPENS IF WE HAVE HEAVY RAINS NEXT YEAR?
WHAT HAPPENS IF TOO MUCH SNOW MELTS ON THE MOUNTAINS IN SPRINGTIME AND RUNS DOWN ONTO THE PLAINS?
YOU ARE A WISE MAN, YU, TO THINK BEYOND THIS DAY OR THE NEXT.
WELL THEN, WISE MAN, **HOW** WILL YOU DEAL WITH RAINS THAT HAVE YET TO FALL AND SNOW THAT HAS YET TO MELT?
A VERY GOOD QUESTION. GIVE ME SOME TIME TO PONDER IT. PERHAPS I WILL FIND AN ANSWER.
HE WILL, YOU KNOW.
WE WILL SEE.

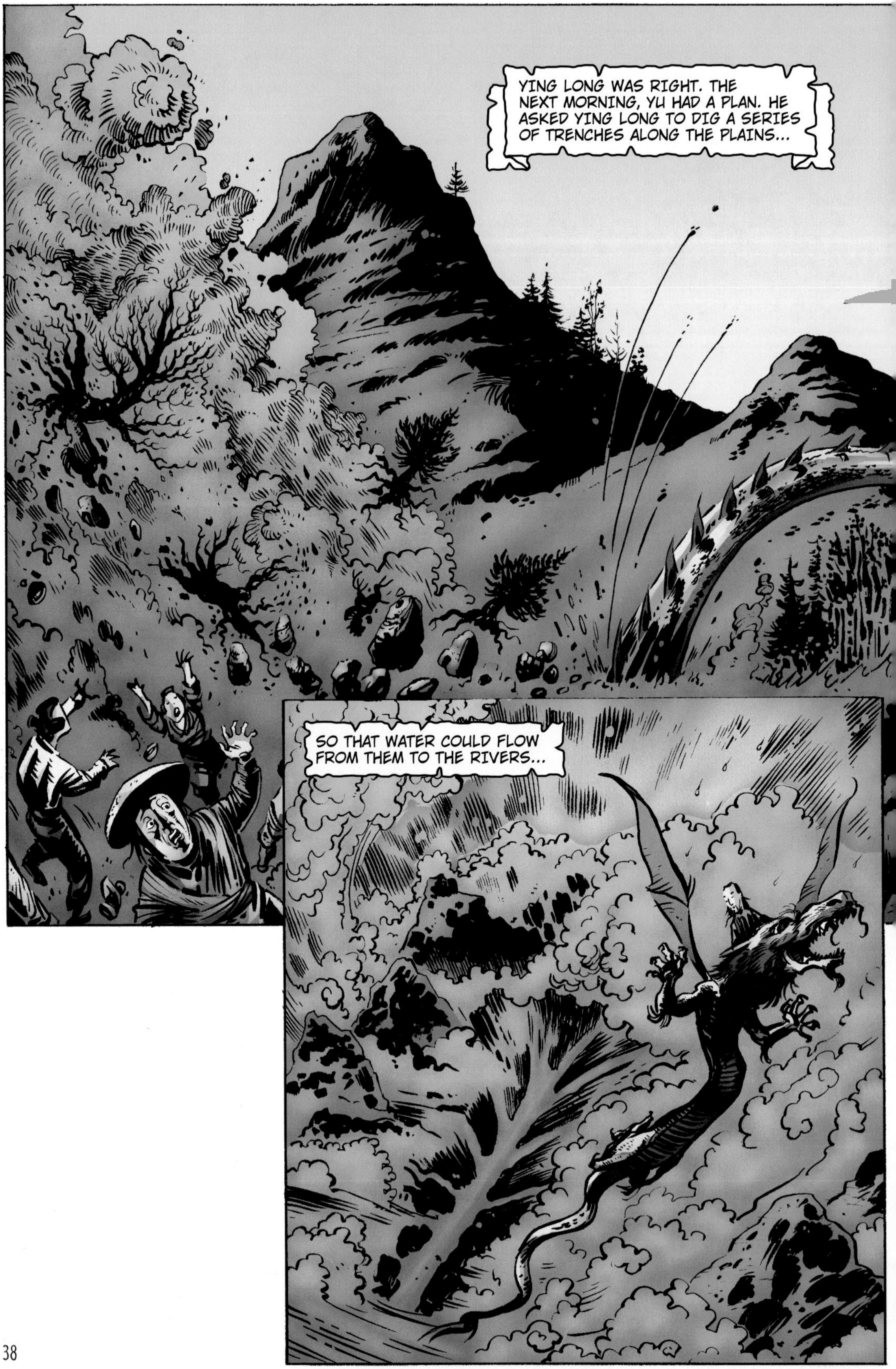
YING LONG WAS RIGHT. THE NEXT MORNING, YU HAD A PLAN. HE ASKED YING LONG TO DIG A SERIES OF TRENCHES ALONG THE PLAINS...
SO THAT WATER COULD FLOW FROM THEM TO THE RIVERS...

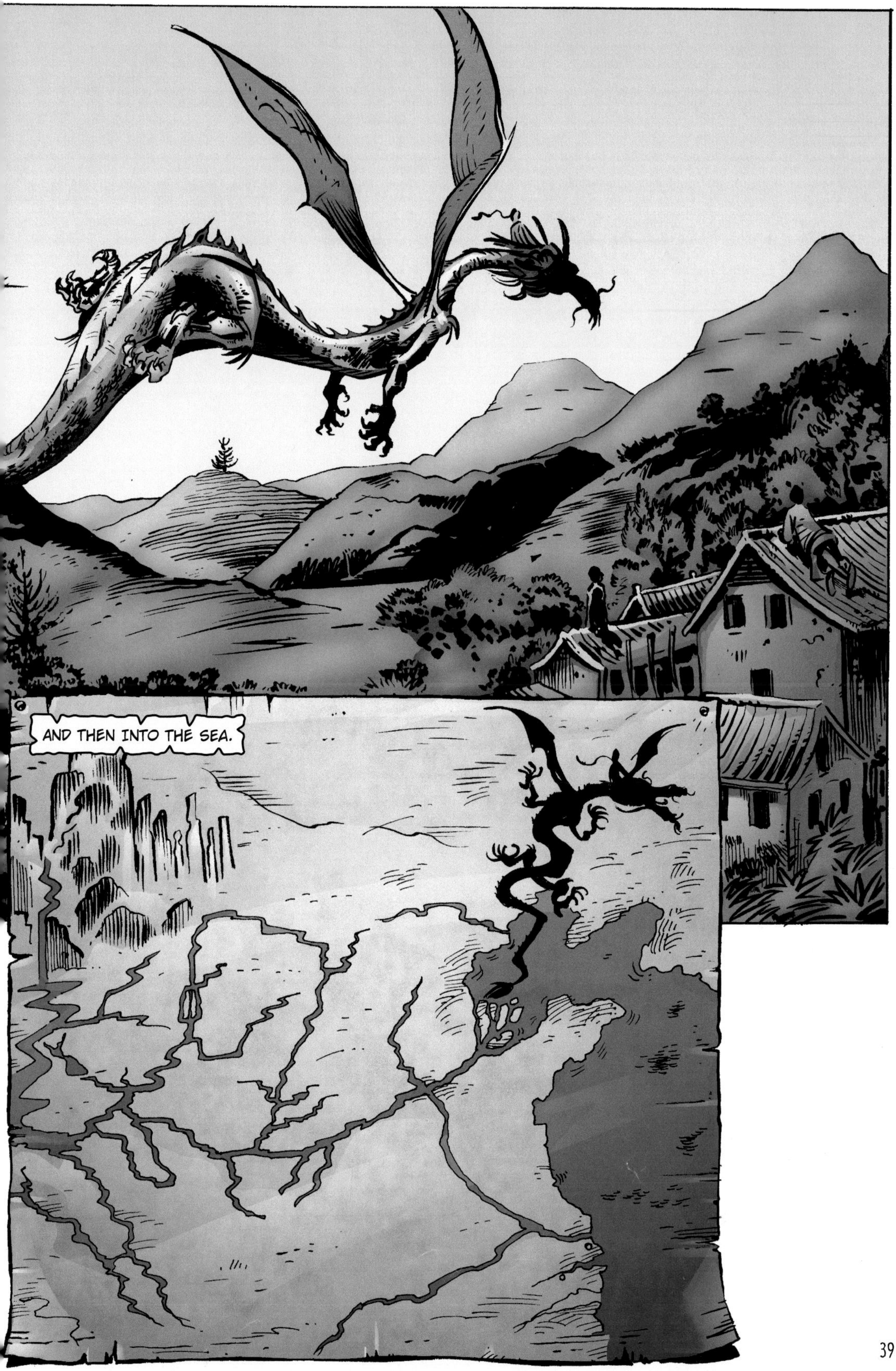
AND THEN INTO THE SEA.

THE MARRIAGE OF YU

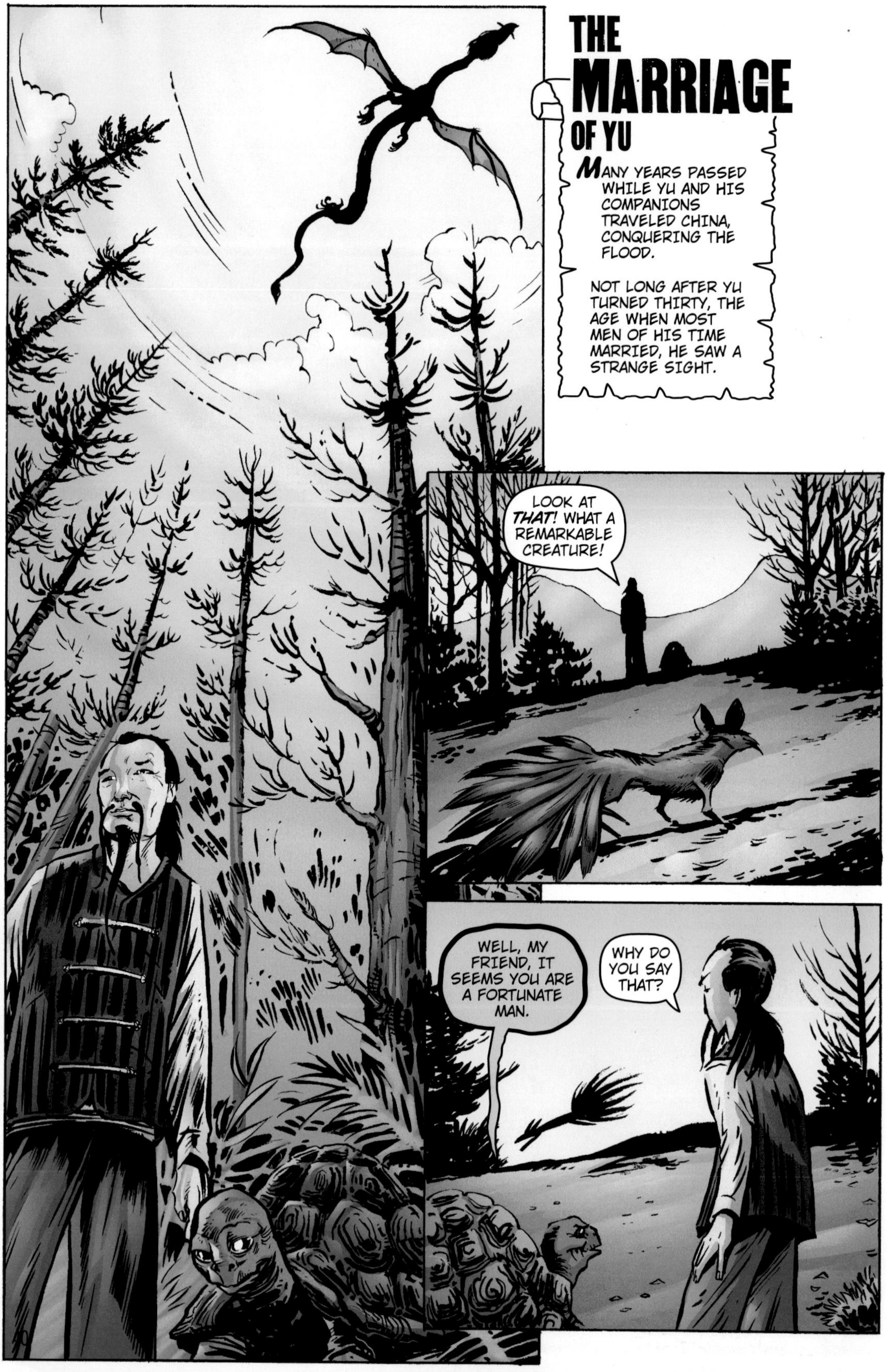
MANY YEARS PASSED WHILE YU AND HIS COMPANIONS TRAVELED CHINA, CONQUERING THE FLOOD.
NOT LONG AFTER YU TURNED THIRTY, THE AGE WHEN MOST MEN OF HIS TIME MARRIED, HE SAW A STRANGE SIGHT.
LOOK AT THAT! WHAT A REMARKABLE CREATURE!
WELL, MY FRIEND, IT SEEMS YOU ARE A FORTUNATE MAN.
WHY DO YOU SAY THAT?

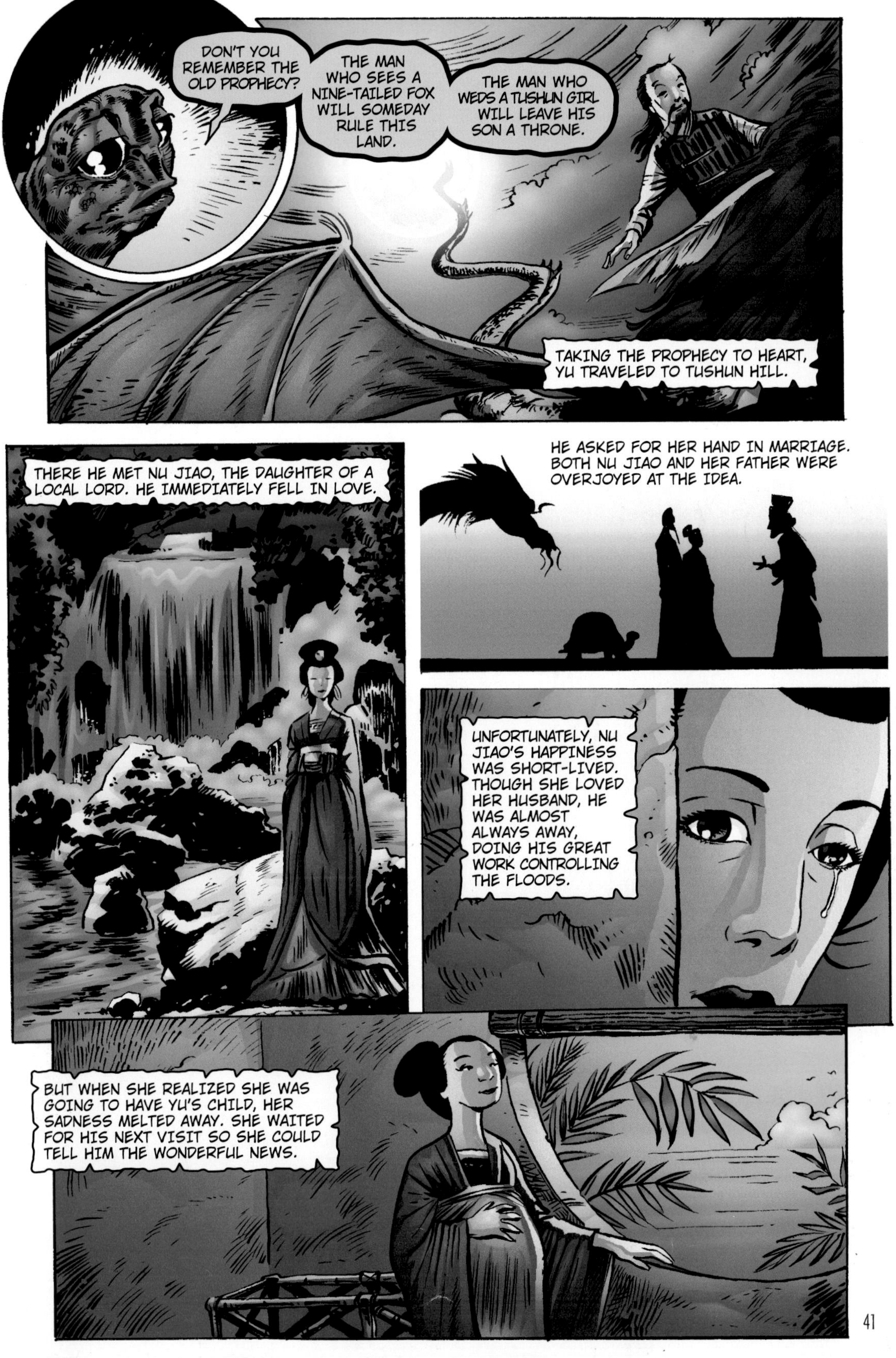
DON'T YOU REMEMBER THE OLD PROPHECY?
THE MAN WHO SEES A NINE-TAILED FOX WILL SOMEDAY RULE THIS LAND.
THE MAN WHO WEDS A TUSHUN GIRL WILL LEAVE HIS SON A THRONE.
TAKING THE PROPHECY TO HEART, YU TRAVELED TO TUSHUN HILL.
THERE HE MET NU JIAO, THE DAUGHTER OF A LOCAL LORD. HE IMMEDIATELY FELL IN LOVE.
HE ASKED FOR HER HAND IN MARRIAGE. BOTH NU JIAO AND HER FATHER WERE OVERJOYED AT THE IDEA.
UNFORTUNATELY, NU JIAO'S HAPPINESS WAS SHORT-LIVED. THOUGH SHE LOVED HER HUSBAND, HE WAS ALMOST ALWAYS AWAY, DOING HIS GREAT WORK CONTROLLING THE FLOODS.
BUT WHEN SHE REALIZED SHE WAS GOING TO HAVE YU'S CHILD, HER SADNESS MELTED AWAY. SHE WAITED FOR HIS NEXT VISIT SO SHE COULD TELL HIM THE WONDERFUL NEWS.

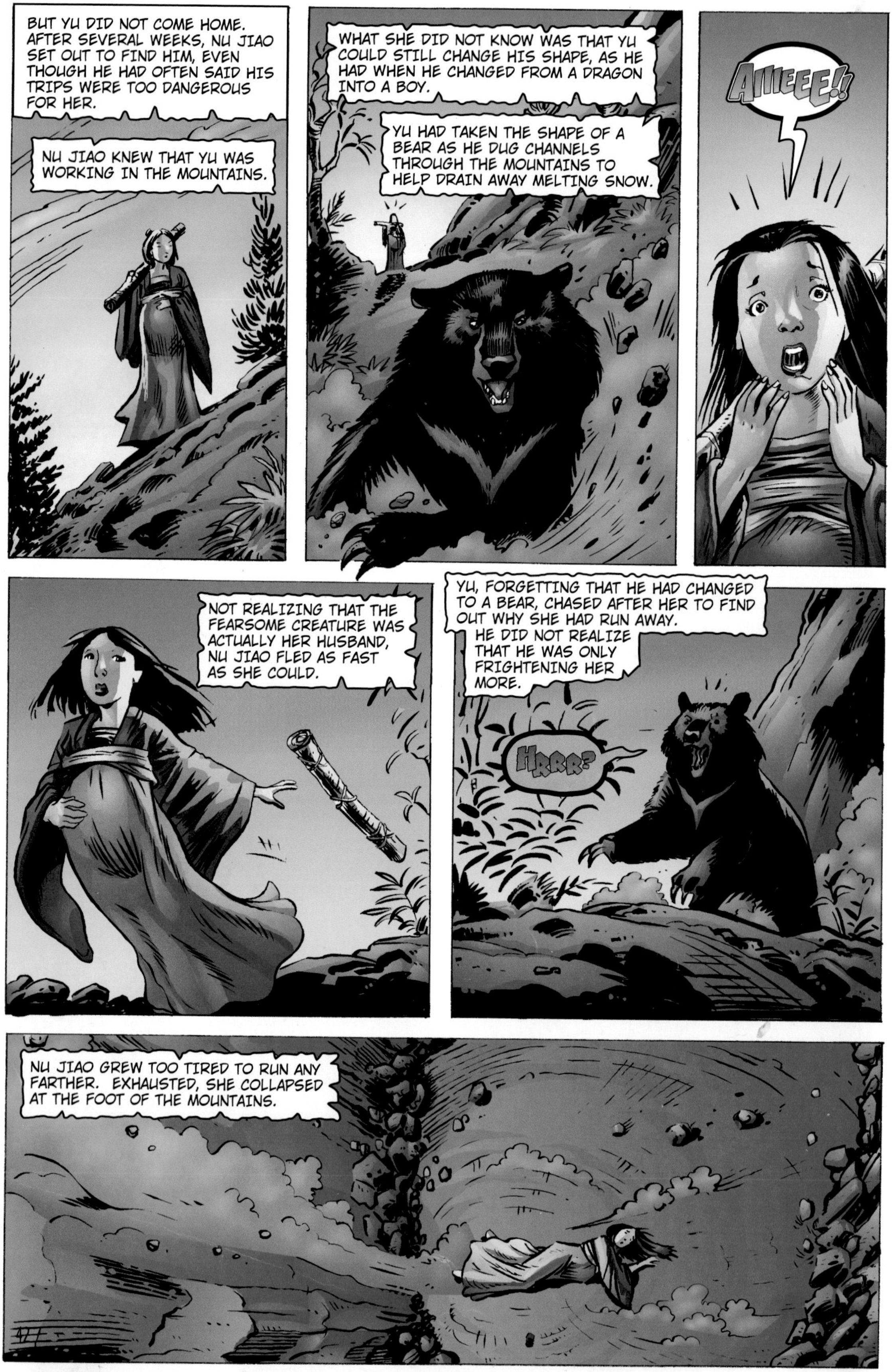
BUT YU DID NOT COME HOME. AFTER SEVERAL WEEKS, NU JIAO SET OUT TO FIND HIM, EVEN THOUGH HE HAD OFTEN SAID HIS TRIPS WERE TOO DANGEROUS FOR HER.
NU JIAO KNEW THAT YU WAS WORKING IN THE MOUNTAINS.
WHAT SHE DID NOT KNOW WAS THAT YU COULD STILL CHANGE HIS SHAPE, AS HE HAD WHEN HE CHANGED FROM A DRAGON INTO A BOY.
YU HAD TAKEN THE SHAPE OF A BEAR AS HE DUG CHANNELS THROUGH THE MOUNTAINS TO HELP DRAIN AWAY MELTING SNOW.
AIIIEEE!!
NOT REALIZING THAT THE FEARSOME CREATURE WAS ACTUALLY HER HUSBAND, NU JIAO FLED AS FAST AS SHE COULD.
YU, FORGETTING THAT HE HAD CHANGED TO A BEAR, CHASED AFTER HER TO FIND OUT WHY SHE HAD RUN AWAY.
HE DID NOT REALIZE THAT HE WAS ONLY FRIGHTENING HER MORE.
HRRR?
NU JIAO GREW TOO TIRED TO RUN ANY FARTHER. EXHAUSTED, SHE COLLAPSED AT THE FOOT OF THE MOUNTAINS.

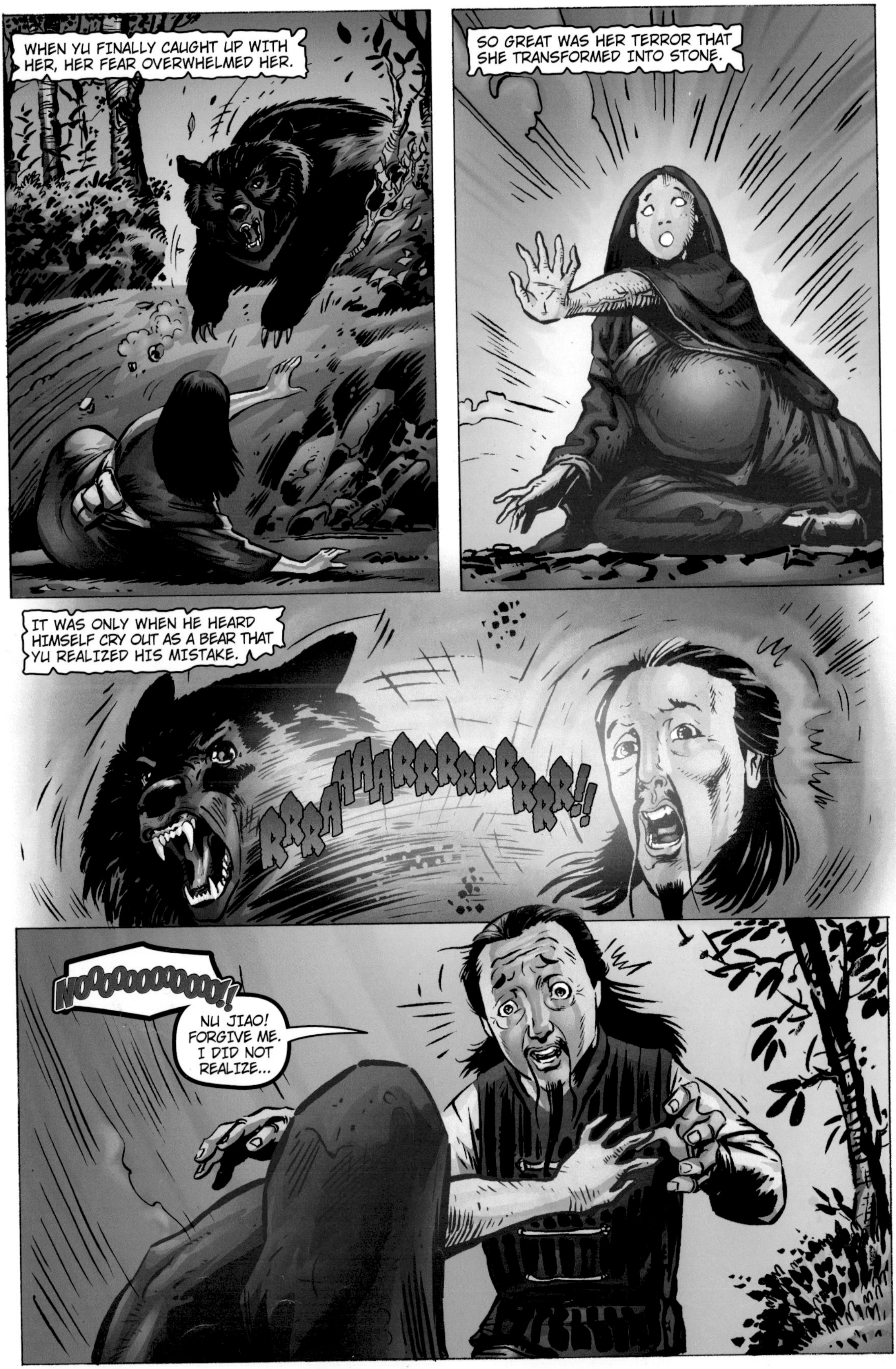
WHEN YU FINALLY CAUGHT UP WITH HER, HER FEAR OVERWHELMED HER.
SO GREAT WAS HER TERROR THAT SHE TRANSFORMED INTO STONE.
IT WAS ONLY WHEN HE HEARD HIMSELF CRY OUT AS A BEAR THAT YU REALIZED HIS MISTAKE.
RRRAAAARRRRRRRRRR!!
NOOOOOOOOOOO!
NU JIAO! FORGIVE ME. I DID NOT REALIZE...

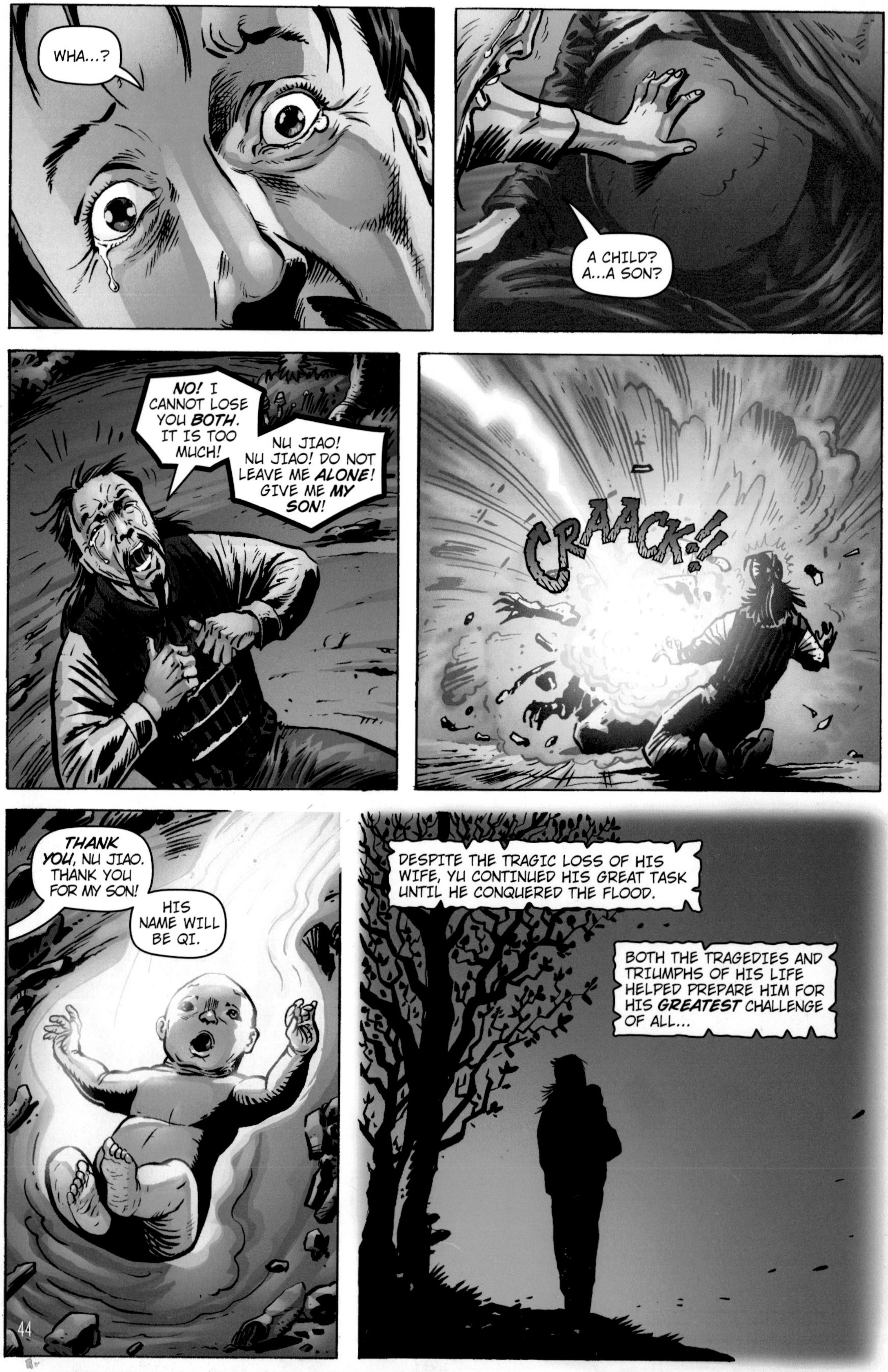
WHA...?
A CHILD? A...A SON?
NO! I CANNOT LOSE YOU BOTH. IT IS TOO MUCH!
NU JIAO! NU JIAO! DO NOT LEAVE ME ALONE! GIVE ME MY SON!
CRAACK!!
THANK YOU, NU JIAO. THANK YOU FOR MY SON!
HIS NAME WILL BE QI.
DESPITE THE TRAGIC LOSS OF HIS WIFE, YU CONTINUED HIS GREAT TASK UNTIL HE CONQUERED THE FLOOD.
BOTH THE TRAGEDIES AND TRIUMPHS OF HIS LIFE HELPED PREPARE HIM FOR HIS GREATEST CHALLENGE OF ALL...

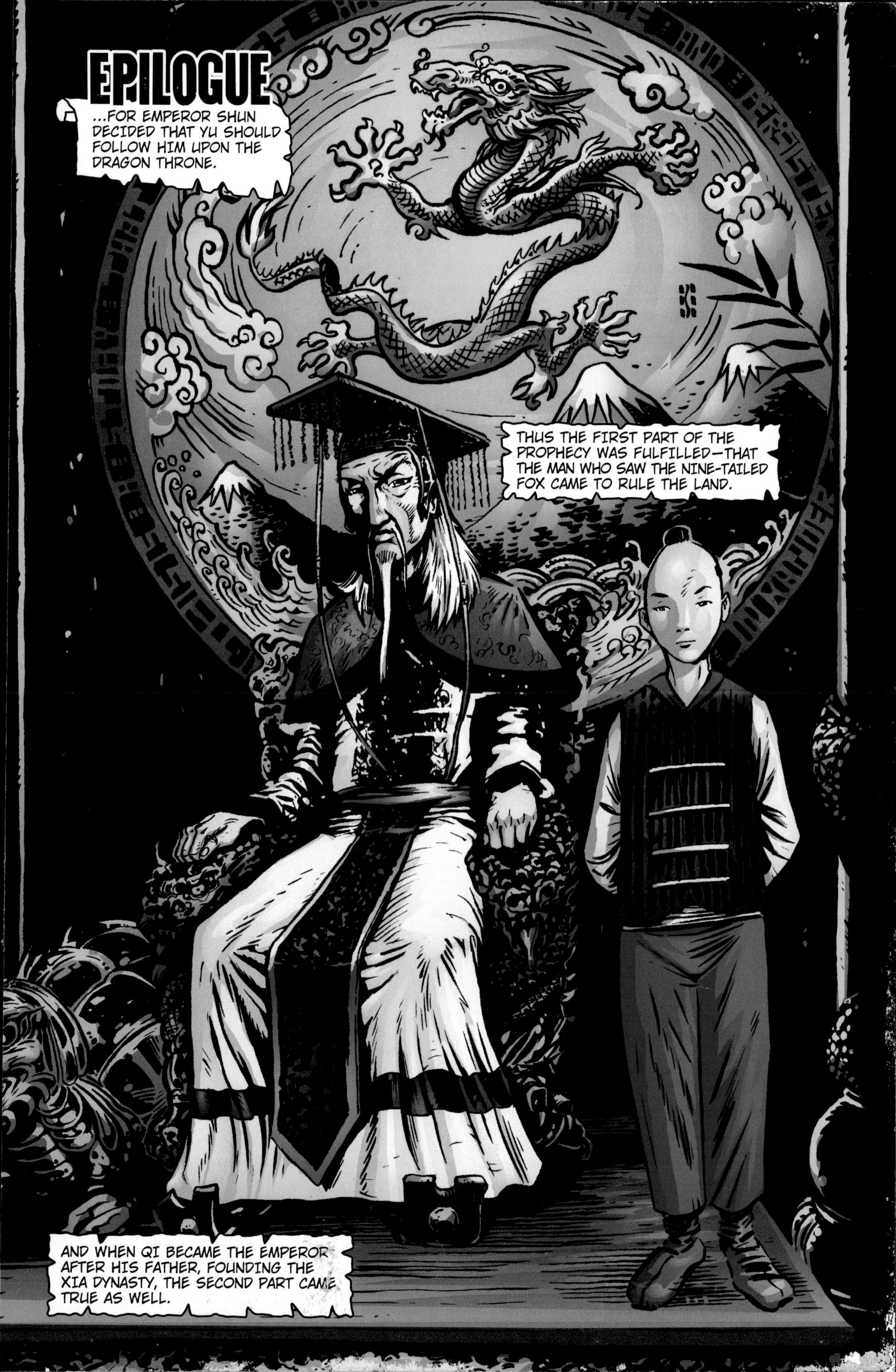
EPILOGUE
...FOR EMPEROR SHUN DECIDED THAT YU SHOULD FOLLOW HIM UPON THE DRAGON THRONE.
THUS THE FIRST PART OF THE PROPHECY WAS FULFILLED—THAT THE MAN WHO SAW THE NINE-TAILED FOX CAME TO RULE THE LAND.
AND WHEN QI BECAME THE EMPEROR AFTER HIS FATHER, FOUNDING THE XIA DYNASTY, THE SECOND PART CAME TRUE AS WELL.

GLOSSARY AND PRONUNCIATION GUIDE

CELESTIAL PALACE: in Chinese myth, the home of the gods, or heaven

DRAGON: in mythology, a magical serpent, often very large. Dragons appear in myths from several countries, but they are very important in China. Dragons appear in Chinese art and literature, on building decorations, and in ceremonies and festivals.

DRAGON THRONE: the traditional seat of Chinese emperors

DYNASTY: a series of kings or emperors, all from the same family, who rule one after another

EMPEROR: the ruler of an empire, or a very large kingdom or territory. In Chinese history, the emperors were believed to be descended from the gods.

GONG GONG (gung gung): the Chinese water god, responsible for storms and flooding

GUN (guhn): a Chinese hero, a grandson of Huang Di and the father of Yu

HUANG DI (hwong *dee*): the Yellow Emperor, the immortal ruler of heaven

IMMORTAL: a person or creature that lives forever. In Chinese myth, immortals can travel between heaven and Earth.

JURONG (*juh*-rung): the Chinese god of fire

NU JIAO (noo je-*ow*): Yu's wife

PROPHECY: a prediction of something to come in the future

QI (chee): Yu's son

SHIRANG (*shee*-rang): in the Yu legend, a magical soil that swells to plug holes and absorb water. Yu uses the shirang to help stop China's floods.

SHUN (shuhn): a Chinese emperor

XIA (*shee*-ah): the first Chinese dynasty described in historical records

YAO (yow): a Chinese emperor

YELLOW EMPEROR: Huang Di, the ruler of heaven. In Chinese culture, the color yellow symbolizes power and authority.

YING LONG (*ying* long): the flying dragon given to Yu by Huang Di

YU (yoo): a Chinese hero, founder of the Xia Dynasty. He is often called Da Yu, a Chinese phrase meaning Yu the Great.

FURTHER READING AND WEBSITES

Behnke, Alison. *China in Pictures*. Minneapolis: Twenty-First Century Books, 2003. This book features information on the history and cultural life of China, from ancient times to the present.

Cheng, Sonia. *Myths and Civilization of the Ancient Chinese*. New York: Peter Bedrick Books, 2001. Cheng retells several major myths, adding historical and cultural details about ancient China.

Chinatown Online, "Yu the Great Conquers the Flood"
http://www.chinatown-online.co.uk/pages/culture/legends/yu.html
The culture section of this website looks at some of the historical roots of the Yu legend.

The National Palace Museum, Taipei, Taiwan
http://www.npm.gov.tw/index.htm
The museum's website features online exhibits of Chinese painting, tapestry, ceramics, and other treasures. The website's Explore and Learn section includes a kids' corner, with interactive pictures of Chinese life.

CREATING *YU THE GREAT*

In creating this story, author Paul Storrie adapted traditional retellings found in *Land of the Dragon: Chinese Myth* (edited by Tony Allan), *An Introduction to Oriental Mythology* (by Clio Whittaker), and other sources on Asian myth. Artist Sandy Carruthers used details from Chinese art, mythology and folklore, museum exhibits, and traditional architecture to shape the story's visual details—from the emperors' robes to the number of toes on Ying Long the dragon. Wang Ping used her knowledge of Chinese culture and history to ensure accuracy.

original pencil from page 9

INDEX

ABOUT THE AUTHOR AND THE ARTIST

PAUL D. STORRIE was born and raised in Detroit, Michigan. He has returned to live there again and again after living in other cities and states. He began writing professionally in 1987 and has written comics for Caliber Comics, Moonstone Books, Marvel Comics, and DC Comics. His work includes *Hercules: The Twelve Labors*, *Amaterasu: Return of the Sun*, *Robin Hood: Outlaw of Sherwood Forest*, *Robyn of Sherwood* (featuring stories about Robin Hood's daughter), *Batman Beyond*, *Gotham Girls*, *Captain America: Red, White and Blue*, and *Mutant X*.

SANDY CARRUTHERS was born in Nova Scotia, Canada. His family moved to Prince Edward Island (PEI), Canada, when he was young. His illustrated published works include *The Men in Black*, *Invaders from Mars*, *Alien Nation*, and *Captain Canuck*. His Web-published works at www.sandycarruthers.com include *The Ronin and the Lily* and *Canadiana: The New Spirit of Canada*. Carruthers currently resides in Charlottetown, PEI, with his partner, Holly; daughter, Eryn; and three cats, Max, Baby, and Harry. He teaches graphic design full-time at Holland College, PEI. Somewhere among all this, he does have a life and will continue his studies of dragons, thanks to Yu.